happiness

AS FOUND IN FORETHOUGHT MINUS FEARTHOUGHT

HORACE FLETCHER

ALICIA EDITIONS

Contents

"HAPPINESS" was written in answer to many questions elicited by the publication of "Menticulture."

The "Introduction" is not material to the subject except to show the sources of the suggestions relative to profitable living contained in the two books.

The vital truths underlying the philosophy of life can be intelligently stated in a few hundred words, both as regards the proper cultivation of the body, or physical equipment, and as regards the cultivation of the mind, so that they may do the best work of which they are capable. False example and false teaching, however, have so impressed habits of weakness on the body and the mind that the chief aim of curative suggestion should be to disabuse. That is, to cause people to discard bad habits of thinking and doing in order that normal, healthy tendencies of action and of thought may take their place.

The difficulty of the task undertaken by any student and advocate of reform is not the intelligent statement of the simple truth, but the discovery and refutation of a complication of errors which have assumed the reality of truth. Simile and illustration, some logic and much ridicule, are among the weapons that have been effective in combating old habits of wrong thinking, but it is impossible to say which argument will fit a particular case.

Each of the illustrations used in this book has been the means of curing some one person of some phase of fearthought, and together they have released many from that dread enemy of health and happiness called "Fear."

The normal condition of Nature is healthy growth—evolution or progression—and Man's chief function in assisting her is first the removal of weeds, or other deterrents to the natural process, and afterwards the maintaining of quarantine against their return.

True Happiness is the Evidence and Fruit of Conscious Usefulness.

The wider the opportunity for usefulness the greater and keener the happiness resulting therefrom. Consciousness of *being* one's best and *doing* one's best, however, regardless of scope, is the only way to unalloyed happiness, and to the accomplishment of the highest ideals. There can be no more miserable, sorry and harrowing condition than that called "Indifference."

The separating of fearthought from forethought is not alone valuable because of the personal comfort of being fearless, but it is especially useful in that the energy made possible by the divorce is available in assisting others to be strong and helpful to themselves and to each other.

If attention is once directed to the pulling of weeds, to the removal of deterrents, to the eradication of the germs of disorder, the pursuit will become most fascinating, owing to the quick and happy response of Nature in her willingness to "Do the rest."

One of the marvels revealed by study of the question of the possibility of a Perfect Social Quarantine, having for its aim a protection that will not permit any child *to escape care*, is the comparatively small areas of the propagating centers in which are bred the germs of social disorder.

This subject is treated in a book, now in press, called "That Last Waif; or, Social Quarantine."

The same insignificance of origin applies to individual, moral and physical deterrents to happiness which afflict otherwise healthy men and women. The *tap-roots* of all unhappiness are not formidable in the light of present knowledge.

Whoever is less than keenly happy is the victim of errors or illusions whose germs are easy to kill when found. It is the especial object of this book to help those who are suffering unhappiness to find the tap-roots of their troubles.

Auditorium Annex, Chicago.

Introduction.

HOW TO BE happy is the one desire common to all humanity.

How to be happier is a better statement, for there is no one so miserable but has some degree of happiness at times—enjoys some moments when he forgets to be unhappy, and looks with appreciation, even if with only dull and bleared appreciation, upon the things that are always beautiful and joyful and free.

In highly civilized life there is everything to encourage, and there should be nothing to prevent, happiness.

The normal condition of man in civilized life is that of happiness.

So great, and so greatly increasing, has been the acceleration of progress, that the possibility of unrestrained and unfettered happiness has come to us in advance of our being prepared to accept the freedom of it, owing, mainly, no doubt, to the weight of traditions under the habit of which we are prone to struggle long after the conditions that gave birth to the traditions have ceased to exist.

The experience of the world has revealed, and is constantly revealing, simple expedients applicable to every possible combination of evils—except the evil of perverse ignorance—the use of which will insure the success of honest and reasonable aims, no matter how unfavorable the equipment and environment have been or are at the present time.

In a singularly adventurous career I have passed through many of the conditions in which discomfort, fear and unhappiness breed, including the direst straits to which life can be exposed, and have also been possessed, at different times, of the means to comfort and happiness that broad opportunity, keen appreciation and affluence are supposed to furnish.

I have shared the occupations and sympathies of persons of many different nationalities and of every degree of opportunity and intelligence; in torrid, temperate and frigid climes; in the Americas, in Africa, in Europe, in Asia, and in the far-off islands of distant seas; on shipboard and on the farm; in the mine and in the factory; in the camp and on the commons; in the arts of war and in the pursuits of peace; in the country cross-roads school-house and in the university; in service and in command—in all of which change it was possible only to serve apprenticeships, however, for in such variety of occupation no great accomplishment could develop, except the accomplishment of variety itself; but, at the same time, it was not possible for any of the occupations to become stale to criticism, and the ability to analyze, in the light of comparison, is the natural result and the impelling motive in these essays.

I have pushed ways through tangled chaparral, led by hopes of discovering precious metals; and have chopped out roads in the jungle, allured by the excitement of the chase and the spirit of adventure. I have observed nature in the vastness of her wild domains; in the calm and in the terror of the mighty deep; in the harmonious quiet of rural cultivation, and in the supreme picturesqueness of rugged mountain landscapes, studded about, here and there, with golden-roofed temples and cloistered parks. I have not only seen nature with appreciative eye when she has displayed her million moods and when she has taken on myriad aspects, but I have tried to interpret her in terms of line and color in famous studios in Europe, under the advice of world-honored masters of the art.

The numerous occupations engaged in were, in many cases, used as necessary means to desired ends. While I have enjoyed making *le grand tour* as a "globe trotter," I have also had to "work my way" at times, and in "working my way" have had to undertake occupations leading that "way." So successful have I been in finding means or excuses for travel, that among my intimates the saying is current that if I "took it into my head" to want to go to either of the poles, I would engage in a business that would make it *necessary* for me to go there, thus conserving my respect for duty and my desire for travel at the same time.

I once sought and secured a place on the staff of one of the great American daily journals in order to gain access to famous studios in Europe and America, and to become acquainted with the personality of great artists who had become inaccessible to anyone except pluto-cratic buyers of works of art, intimate friends and critics. This was while I was studying art with a view to learning some of the secrets of its inspiration in practice, and thus journalism served a useful purpose, as well as satisfied a burning curiosity. In this connection I will say that I have since been able, directly and indirectly, to create appreciation that has led to the purchase of works of art in which very large sums of money have been involved, so that I cannot be charged with imposture upon a profession which I respect to the point of reverence for its mission in holding a "true mirror up to nature" and in teaching us to appreciate the subtle beauties that nature shows in all of her aspects, but which become commonplace to the many without the assistance of art.

The Japanese have a proverb which declares that "once seeing is better than an hundred times telling about," and this good proverb has been the guiding star of my roamings, and has suggested prac-tical participation in some of my occupations. My first attempt to see the antipodes was not successful. It did not have the necessary parental sanction, and I was *brought back* before I had measured very much longitude and latitude; but the determination shown in the attempt indicated so strong a tendency that it led to promise of assistance and permission to travel as a reward for certain accom-plishments in study that were considered to be impossible, as judged by former efforts, but which became surprisingly easy to the boy who saw a way to the other side of the world in the task.

I spent my sixteenth birthday on the Island of Java, and saw Japan and China at the most interesting periods of their recent history—Japan, in Feudal Times, before any of the changes that have made her the last and greatest wonder of the world; and China, at the close of the Taiping rebellion, wherein more than thirty millions of persons lost their lives, and about which there hovered a lawlessness the like of which the world has not witnessed elsewhere.

Chance and restless change have thrown me into companionship with the most elemental of human beings; and have also led me to the acquaintance, and into the affections of the wisest and loveliest of men and women—the rarest blossoms of our generation. Opportunity has found me available for the command of a crew of Cantonese pirates, on a Chinese lorcha, at a time when piracy was a common occupation in the China Sea; and for the mismanagement of a French Grand Opera Company, when no one else was foolish enough to undertake it.

The foregoing are but glimpses of the opportunities for observation out of which I draw my deductions relative to profitable living. Four complete trips around the world—two of them before the time of ocean steamship lines and continental railroads; thirty-six trips across the American Continent by various rail, water and stage routes; sixteen voyages across the Pacific Ocean, and many across the Atlantic; intermittent periods of residence in many different countries of Europe, in China, in India, in Japan and in different localities in the Americas; as well as visits to parts remote from the lines of travel, such as South Africa, Yucatan and the mountain regions of Mexico and Central America, that are the type of all of the South American countries; and all of which residences and visits have been chosen at times of greatest interest in each locality; in response to the invitation of the Spirit-of-Adventure by which I have been led— these, together with no less than thirty-eight distinct occupations, embrace the sum of my opportunities.

Fortune has always been kind to me when I have trusted her; when my aims and ambitions were worthy, and when I have been sufficiently appreciative and grateful for the things I already possessed to merit and invite continued favors; but, she has always passed me by whenever I have doubted her goodness or questioned her intentions. And so consistent has been the course of Fortune, as viewed in the retrospect, that I can assert, with all the assurance of firm belief, that "Unto him who hath (appreciation and gratitude) shall be given; but unto him who hath not (appreciation and gratitude) shall be taken away even that which he hath."

Until I began to collect my remembrances into groups, form them into classes for review and deduct from them suggestions for profitable living, I had thought that my chronic restlessness was aimless as measured by the common estimate of usefulness; but the sympathy aroused by the publication of my little volume—first, privately printed,—*Menticulture, or the A-B-C of True Living*— revealed the possibility of utilizing my varied experiences and observations to good advantage in calling attention to uses-of-energy, points-of-view, habits-of-thought and habits-of-action, that made for happiness in some persons in some parts of the world, while they were entirely unknown to others as well fitted to enjoy them.

I was led to serious study of the causes and effects of happiness and unhappiness by observations of the pitiable neglect of the science of menticulture, (which is the science of fundamental means), and the science of happiness (which is the science of ultimate desirable ends), in materially civilized communities, and by persons who have mastered, and are already possessed of, the physical means to comfort and happiness. This neglect is not surprising when we reflect that all available time and all available thought have been excitedly employed in developing material, physical *means*, to the exclusion of the thought of cultivating the end; to the harnessing and training of the forces of Nature, to the exclusion of planning for their best uses; but it will be surprising if, however, in the near future, the ends are not scientifically cultivated, now that the fundamental as well as the physical means are understood, and the leisure to apply them is secured.

More than forty years of observation, and upwards of three years of study, analysis and arrangement with a fixed purpose, have enabled me to suggest changes of attitude towards the problems of life that have not failed to bring more or less strength and happiness to all who have adopted them, as attested by thousands of written and verbal communications and by report. This is literally true, and the statement of it is warranted by the merit of the results, removed from any personality in connection with it.

The underlying cause of all weakness and unhappiness in Man, heredity and environment to the contrary notwithstanding, has always been, and is still, *weak habit-of-thought*. This is proven by the observed instances in which *strong habit-of-thought* has invariably made its masters superior to heredity, and to environment, and to illness, and to weakness of all kinds, and has redeemed them from non-success and misery, to the enjoyment of success, honor and happiness. It has also been proven that none are so ill-favored as to be exempt from regeneration by the influence of optimistic thinking, and none so plain, nor even so ugly, as judged by the world's standards of beauty, but that the radiance of pure thought will make them more beautiful than their brothers of nobler mien and more symmetrical physique, but whose thoughts are poisoned by fear and by selfishness.

Happiness is not dependent upon wealth, and wealth does not necessarily bring happiness, but both are dependent upon *good-habit-of-thought*; for *good-habit-of-thought* develops *appreciation*, which is the measure of all wealth, and *appreciation* leads to the *habit-of-feeling* and the *habit-of-action* which produce happiness.

Notwithstanding the words of Jesus of Nazareth, by which one-half of the world's inhabitants are supposed to be governed; notwithstanding the admonitions of the other great teachers to whom the other half of humanity turn for counsel; notwithstanding the lessons taught by all of nature's processes of growth, especially the teachings of later evolution; fear—fear of death, fear of disaster, fear of non-attainment, fear of non-preferment, and fear of the things that never happen as feared, and the anger and the worry growing out of these fears—have been looked upon as afflictions necessary to humanity, repressible only during life, and eradicable only at the change called death.

Early theology wrestled with conditions wherein it was thought necessary to use the whip of fear as well as the attraction of love to incline men to religion. Modern theology teaches the religion of love alone, but it has not yet sufficiently denounced the former teaching of fears, perhaps in the interest of consistency or because of filial respect, inasmuch as its parents once put the label of *truth* upon the religion of fear. Science also has taught, and still continues to teach, the potency of the *crowding-out* stimulant in growth, without proclaiming a line where attraction became the stronger motive in civilization—an intangible line already far astern in the wake of present progress.

Fear has had its uses in the evolutionary process, and seems to constitute the whole of forethought, as instinct seems to constitute the whole of intelligence in most animals, but that it should remain any part of the mental equipment of human civilized life is an absurdity. There are, undoubtedly, human beings that are still so nearly animal that fear alone will restrain them from wrong-doing, or stimulate them (or, rather, *push* them) to peaceful and useful living, but none such will read this book, and neither you nor I should be burdened by their limitations or necessities. We have passed the point where we need to be *pushed*; or, if we have not, we are ashamed to confess it, thereby acknowledging that it is unnecessary; and are within the atmosphere of appreciation and attraction where fear and its expressions have no proper place, and where the toleration of fear beclouds not only our own clear vision, but also the vision of those who are still below us in the scale of intelligence, to whom, as beacon-lighters on the heights above them, we owe the influence of right example.

I have made especial study of the reports of the Society for Psychical Research, the book entitled "Fear," by Prof. Angelo Mosso, of Turin, Italy, and the contributions to the *American Journal of Psychology* by President G. Stanley Hall, of Clarke University, Worcester, Massachusetts; Dr. Colin A. Scott, Professor of Psychology and Child Study at Cook County Normal School, Chicago, Illinois; and others who are devoting particular attention to the causes and effects of fears in children; together with the after-effect of early fears upon persons when they are fully grown. The claim of these students is that the consideration of the future that constitutes *forethought* is a mixture of hope, faith and fear, the sum of which is the stimulant to action and progress, hope and faith being the civilized or divine motives, and fear being the animal motive. My own experience and observations corroborate this contention, but I find that the fear element of forethought is *not* stimulating to the more civilized persons, to whom duty and attraction are the natural motives of stimulation, but is weakening and deterrent. As soon as it becomes unnecessary, fear becomes a positive deterrent, and should be entirely removed, as dead flesh is removed from living tissue. I have also demonstrated, beyond the possibility of doubt, that *the fear element can be eliminated* out of forethought *as soon as it becomes evident that it is unnecessary, separable and eliminable*, and that *energy* and *desire* for progress and growth *are beautifully stimulated as the result of its elimination.*

To assist in the analysis of fear, and in the denunciation of its expressions, I have coined the word *"fearthought"* to stand for the unprofitable element of forethought, and have defined that variously-interpreted word "worry" as *fearthought, in contradistinction to forethought.* I have also defined "fearthought" as the *self-imposed* or *self-permitted* suggestion of *inferiority*, in order to place it where it really belongs, in the category of harmful, unnecessary, and, therefore, not-respectable things.

Darwin and Spencer and other biologists have asserted that if primitive man had not been urged by fear of discomfort he would have sat upon a stone, naked, near the roots or the herbs that served to appease his hunger—if it also happened to be near to a spring where he could quench his thirst—until he died; and that fear has been the impelling motive in the progress of the race. This was undoubtedly true up to a certain point, but, like many of the laws of *ye olden tyme*, is not applicable to the present nor to us.

There is now sufficient protection vouchsafed by forethought, and sufficient attraction furnished by affection and duty, to lead the van in the pursuit of progress, and to set an example that will be its own torch-bearer in guiding the trend of thought and of action.

When the motto, "Fearlessness," becomes embroidered upon the banners of all of our religious and other fraternal organizations; when "Freedom from Fear" becomes the slogan of Reform, and when Appreciation, Love and Altruism are admitted to the councils of men, then, and only then, will famine end, selfishness fade, strikes become unnecessary, misery depart, and Happiness become enthroned as the ruler of a joyously industrious and universally prosperous people.

Increase is prodigal, and accumulation is already prodigious, so that it is no longer a question of physical means, but a question of wise distribution and adjustment, to accomplish all that society requires to insure it unremitting happiness.

Churches there are, clubs there are, lodges there are, guilds there are, and many other fraternal organizations whose aims are practically the same, but whose members are attracted together into separate groups by sympathies of traditions, race, occupations or general trend-of-thought. It would be a useless iconoclasm to separate from these or to attempt to dismember them. They are all good organizations, wherein they conserve the principles of brotherhood and promote practical altruism; and are only imperfect wherein they tolerate slavery to the fears, slavery to wealth, slavery to the harmful conventions, and slavery to the antagonisms, intolerances and other evil passions that prevent economic co-operation, harmony and happiness.

The contention of this book is that, with means already secured, there is a way to individual happiness, *even under existing conditions*; and also, that the present acceleration of progress, and certain already accomplished tests of possible industrial and economic reform, coupled with an optimism that has for its motto, "All *can be*, and, therefore, *shall be* well," not only promise, but assure, to mankind, in a not remote future, equal opportunities for securing happiness by means altogether honest and altruistic.

To *all* who will follow me through this volume, I promise to show ways and signs that will assist the weak to become strong, the poor to become rich in appreciation of their opportunities, and the rich to better enjoy their good fortune without impoverishing others to do so. My special desire is to enlist general aid in eradicating deterrents to growth, and in the acceleration of progress.

Hypothesis.

THE OBJECT of Life is Growth.

Harmony is the condition favorable and necessary to growth.

Harmony is the normal condition of Nature, as proven by the unfailing and immediate response of growth to its influence.

Harmonic conditions are created by the removal of deterrents to growth.

Mind is the first essential in the growth of Man. A healthy mind insures a healthy body, and a rational cultivation of the mind cannot fail to result in the attainment of the highest ideals.

All of the processes of Nature are consistent, and Man and Mind are no exception to the rule regulating the growth of other things, except that their functions as chief assistants in evolution are unique, and, therefore, involve greater responsibility.

Unselfishness is necessary to the harmonic condition in Man, and service to fellow-man is essential to his growth.

Happiness is the evidence and fruit of Growth.

There can be no real happiness except in Growth.

Acts are thoughts materialized; or—thoughts realized.

Forethought is an essential aid to Growth.

Fearthought is the cause of all deterrents to growth in Man.

Forethought minus Fearthought is the ideal Mind Equipment.

Fearthought serves no useful purpose; neither is it a necessary infliction of intelligent, civilized manhood or womanhood.

———

Culture is necessary to the best growth.

Mind-culture, or *menticulture*, is the most important of all the divisions of culture; for, out of Mind thoughts spring, and accomplishments grow; but it has been the last to receive the same scientific and reasonable attention that the other cultures have received, and had not even been given a distinctive name until *Menticulture* was published.

In Agriculture and in Horticulture, plants that seem to have no profitable nor agreeable use, but are deterrent to the growth of useful plants, are denominated "weeds," and are not allowed to retain root in the same soil; animals and other living and moving things that are not serviceable, and can not be domesticated, are exterminated from civilized environment; the air that Man breathes is cleared of poisonous malaria by draining the swamps in which the bad air forms; and friction is minimized in machines, in order that the energy applied to them may meet with least resistance, and suffer the least waste. But no such care is commonly given to the mind.

Fearthought is the element of friction, as expressed in anger; it is the predatory element, as expressed in waste of energy—the result of worry; and it is also the weed element, as shown by the uselessness of it in any form. It is, however, permitted to encumber, muddy and prey upon divinely ordained forethought, as weeds encumber good soil, as mud clouds pure water, and as savage and venomous things prey upon the comfort and life of animals useful to Man, and even upon Man himself.

Man's place in the process of evolution is that of assistant only. Man selects, arranges, brings together, separates, waters, fertilizes, waits upon and otherwise cultivates Nature; but he has not been able to add one cell to growth; neither has he succeeded in drawing an atom of color from the sunlight and in infusing it into the sap of any growing thing.

By Man's attention in removing the deterrents, the skimpy little wild flower that grows upon the hillsides of China, that I gathered when I was a boy—of less importance than the common field daisy—has become the royal chrysanthemum of the Flower Shows; by Man's care in the breeding, feeding and training of the primitive horse described by Professor Marsh, the almost-human Kentucky thoroughbred—the "Black Beauty" of our pride—has been evolved; and the clumsy effort of the first inventor of steam applied to machinery has become the wonderful quadruple-expansion engine of the present, by the harmonizing adjustment of parts, and the reduction of friction to the point of noiseless efficiency, through the genius of invention.

Mind is the great machine behind all other machines and out of which all accomplishment comes. Fearthought and what grows out of it, under the class names of anger and worry, are like rust and sand in the journals, and wear out the bearings of the machine. They are also like the impurities in water that cause foaming in a boiler and prevent the accumulation of energy. They are productive of nothing but wear and waste, *wear and waste*, as long as they are permitted to encumber the splendid man-machine and its source of power.

The creative—the growing part—of Nature never fails to do her part if the deterrents to growth are removed. What she does for the growth of plants and of animals, and for the creation of power from the use of her forces called steam and electricity, she will also do for the growth and development of the mind of man. If fearthought and its various expressions are eradicated; or, more correctly speaking, are not sought and nursed, as they always are, nothing can prevent Growth and Service and Happiness from occupying their own; and if the carbonic-acid-gas of passion is kept out of the mental atmosphere, a vitalized, altruistic and spiritualized energy will take its place. *Good comes to whatever is prepared for it.*

It is an easy matter to separate fearthought from forethought if it is known that they are separable; not by suppression, nor by process of gradual repression; because, as long as a spark of fearthought remains, any excitement or draft of surprise may revive the flame to destructive proportions; but by absolute eradication,—determination not to suffer, nor permit, nor tolerate.

The method of eradication is, by the way, the method that is easier than not, as soon as conviction of the possibility of it is nursed into a belief.

Effective methods are always easy methods.

Repression acknowledges, and therefore strengthens, the evil to be repressed, is never-ending and altogether ineffectual.

Eradication is the simple method of ceasing to import or admit evil counsel or report, and is the only effective method in menticulture.

While the future is the field in which growth must take place, the now or, rather, the immediate-next-future, is the *only* time for action. Are you possessed of fearthought, or anger, or worry, or suspicion, or jealousy, or envy, or malice, or indifference at this moment? No! You cannot be, for two distinct thoughts cannot occupy the mind at the same time, and your thought is occupied with the subject matter of this hypothesis. The next time you have any of these poisons you will have to import them afresh in response to the invitation of so mean a liar as Suspicion, or at the command of so silly a coward as Fear. Habit-of-thought-of-evil—*the devil*—will return to you for the usual easy conquest, but newly-acquired knowledge of his impotency to harm can aid Determination to resist him until Habit-of-Thought is no longer Bad-Habit-of-Thought and will, therefore, no longer assist in the materialization of the spook. And then, and *only* then, will you be free—free to grow, eager to serve, and altogether happy.

All time—all eternity—is made up of a succession of *nows*. If you are free in the present *now*, you may more easily be free from temptation in the succeeding *nows* until emancipation shall be complete and the very atmosphere of your freedom shall exorcise all evil before it can come near enough to attract your consciousness.

You are free this moment; you can be free in the succeeding moments; *you can be free forever!* It is easier than not!

Theory.

THE PERFECT MAN is the harmonious man.

Perfection in man is attained when he is *doing his best.*

Symmetry of face or of form, quality of voice, or strength of mind or muscle at birth are the responsibility of the Creator and of progenitors.

The birth of the body of man is accomplished when it attains consciousness of its physical requirements.

The birth of the soul of man is accomplished when he attains consciousness of what is good, of what his functions and duties are relative to his own best growth, and also relative to his uses and duties as a member of society.

Man is not fully born until his mind is conscious of his body and conscious of his soul, and knows the functions and duties of each relative to the best growth.

Until man is fully born, as described above, the responsibility of his perfection or imperfection rests with his teachers and their teachings.

Everything that man is conscious of is his teacher.

You are the teacher of every person who sees or is otherwise conscious of you or of your example.

It is unmanly, and especially unchristian, not to seek the greatest possible enlightenment relative to the functions and duties in growth, not only for your own sake, but as an example for others; and, being enlightened, not to do all possible to assist growth.

Whoever reads and assents to the above, takes upon himself the responsibility of his future growth, and will be respectable or not-respectable insofar as he seeks enlightenment and assists growth, or neglects to seek enlightenment and thereby retards growth.

Happiness, the evidence, fruit and reward of growth, rests in self-respect first, and, incidentally, in the measure of respect held by others.

No one is respectable who is not *doing his best.*

When a man finds fault with the material with which he has been furnished—with his form, with his face, with his mind, with his muscle, with his equipment of wealth, or other means or tools of growth, at the time of his being fully born, he puts blame upon, and thereby blasphemes, his Creator, as well as discredits his progenitors.

Whoever reads, and assents to, the foregoing is fully born, in that he has learned and now *knows what is best.* The question then is: "What will he do with it?"

In highly-civilized life it is *not-respectable not to be fully born.*

The fully-born *is not doing his best,* and is therefore *not-respectable when he suffers himself to retain or cultivate the habit-of-fearthought.*

The fully-born is *not doing his best,* and therefore is *not-respectable, when he entertains and nurses worry.*

The fully-born is *doing his worst when he allows himself to be angry.*

The fully-born is unmanly, especially unchristian and altogether not-respectable when he is not doing his best, and is always a subject for pity, and frequently a subject for contempt, when he is doing his worst.

The fully-born-and-entirely-respectable individual knows that fearthought is an unprofitable element of forethought, knows that it can be eliminated from the habit-of-feeling by persistent, intelligent habit-of-thought, and, knowing this, prepares the field of his mind for unhampered growth by eradicating all of the expressions of fearthought, as well as all other deterrents to growth.

The fully-born-and-entirely-respectable individual is the one to whom come health, strength, memory, inspiration, love, preferment, altruistic impulses, and the appreciation necessary to find the greatest enjoyment in them all.

The fully-born-and-entirely-respectable individual needs not symmetry of form nor beauty of face nor accumulation of wealth to make him happy, for the light from within will give grace to his form, reflect beauty from his face, and attract all of the things that constitute wealth.

The fully-born-and-entirely-respectable condition is the condition that is easier than not, pleasanter than any, and in which only true happiness dwells.

Out of the fully-born-and-entirely-respectable habit-of-being and habit-of-thinking, nursed within our professedly-altruistic organizations, will the impulse spring which will so shape conditions that unhappiness can no longer exist, except as the result of perversity.

Prefatory definitions.

MUCH MISUNDERSTANDING ARISES from the various interpretations of the meaning of terms. So different are the interpretations given to some words, that a large part of the dictionaries is taken up with synonyms whose varied applications are nearly as wide apart as the limits of the greatest misunderstanding.

Many of these different applications of words are the result of corruptions of the original meaning, but they are none the less misleading, and furnish an excuse for agreeing on specific definitions.

As an example of corrupt uses given to words that should be held to convey only a sacred meaning, take the word "love," as promiscuously applied, for instance. It should be removed from all selfishness, and attach only to such holy application as that implied by the expression, "God is Love." In its application to individuals, as in mother-love, child-love, love between husband and wife, or between brothers, it should only have spiritual significance, unalloyed by any suggestion of liking, approval, desire, or lust; and should even extend its mantle to spread alike over all created things.

Love had already been so corrupted in its uses in the time of Comte, that he was impelled to coin a new word to express unselfishness between brother-men, and hence gave the word "altruism"—(other-self)—to the world.

"Altruism," also, in its turn, has suffered by contact with the selfish habit-of-thought of the present time, until it does not longer express the highest quality of love—the spiritual—but rather the socio-commercial quality that seeks and expects reward of praise or material emolument.

Although it is some time since "altruism" was first used—and it is a word of most important meaning to sociology—there are few who can define it.

Probably the material rush of the time has allowed little opportunity for acquaintance with it. It is rarely seen in the magazines, and almost never in the daily papers. This is probably the reason why the author was able to find only three, out of thirty persons asked, who could define "altruism." These thirty were met haphazard, and represented a fair average of city intelligence. It follows, by inference, that there is not as much altruism as there should be in existence among us, for, if there were, the word chosen by Comte to express it would be more widely used and known.

In presenting a set of definitions, there is no intention of calling into question the intelligence of any reader. The idea was suggested by the wide difference of understanding of the meaning of the word "worry." This difference of understanding became apparent in the discussion of *Menticulture*.[*]

It was found that many persons defined "worry" as "any consideration of the future," whereas only apprehensive consideration of the future was intended to be meant by its use in *Menticulture*.

Reference to the origin of the word revealed that it was first used to express the "barking of a small dog," probably in contradistinction to the biting of a large dog. It was first "worrit," and became "worry," as now, later on. "Picking" and "nagging" were its synonyms in slang until they were taken into the language as sober expressions.

In the attempt to separate "worry" from "forethought," the word

---

[*] *Menticulture* is the title of a book by the present author, whose mission is to declare a theory of the possible and very profitable eradication of the germs of all evil, and consequent unhappiness, which are commonly assembled under the class names of "anger" and "worry",—"anger" representing the aggressive, and "worry" representing the cowardly passions.

"fearthought" was coined, and hence our present title, and also the definitions hereunder, whose object is to render misunderstanding as nearly impossible as possible.

Only a few of the words relative to our treatise are defined—only such as have been found to cause discussion in consideration of the subject.

GOD

No definition of the Christian conception of God can be adequate. God is the source of all, in all, and around all. "The Absolute," "Father," "Creator," "Jehovah," "Source" and other terms are used for euphony and to express separate God-qualities. Whoever attempts to define God, shows pitiful limitations thereby. We may *feel* God, but we cannot *define* God. *Appreciation* of God is the measure of man's possibilities of growth and the key to power and happiness.

APPRECIATION

Even in its material application, "appreciation" is a word of greatest importance, and should mean *the highest form of intelligence*. It is commonly used to express only a simple knowledge of value, but it should have a larger significance, by conveying the idea of fullest cultivation and enjoyment as well as knowledge.

Wealth, for instance, can be measured only by appreciation. The child in appreciating a toy is richer than a drowning man with a thousand dollars in gold in his pocket. We will therefore understand appreciation to mean *knowledge and full cultivation and enjoyment*.

"Appreciation" might justly be given first place in the language, as, in its spiritual application, it implies the knowledge of God that gives birth to Love.

Our definition, "knowledge—or understanding—cultivation and full enjoyment," conveys the largest and highest meaning of "appreciation," but the realization of it is not complete until every God-expression is included, even to the smallest wonder of the universe.

Neglect of the cultivation of appreciation of *everything*—of the commonest things in our surroundings—is loss of opportunity to conserve the greatest aid to progress and growth; because, appreciation of lesser things insures a better appreciation of the most important things.

Cultivation of appreciation is cultivation of the germ of all good and the opening wide of the spiritual flood-gates. Even the complete, yet simple, dignity of the Lord's Prayer can be epitomized within the prayer, *Father, teach Thou us Appreciation.*

LOVE

In its pure form, as Christ meant it, Love makes no distinction between creatures nor between things; its merit is in the act—or thought—and not in the object loved.

The divine quality in man, growing out of appreciation, finds first expression in love; not the passive principle, the opposite of hate, but the growing, active principle, which is constantly flowing forth from the spiritually blessed to bathe with warmth of unselfishness the just and the unjust alike. Love begets altruism.

As "perfect love casteth out fear," so does the eradication of fear insure the wooing of perfect love.

ALTRUISM

Next in the scale of importance is Comte's word "altruism," which was coined to suggest the Christ-like attitude of unselfish service between fellow-men. It is, however, as before stated, now commonly understood to be the social or business application of the principle of love which needs and expects to be reciprocal. Men were asked to become altruists when they were asked to "do unto others as you would that others should do unto you." Growth towards divinity is the fruit of perfect altruism. Perfect Love begets Perfect Altruism. Christ is the Perfect Altruist.

SPONTANEOUS ALTRUISM

Any degree of altruism is good and is sure to lead to higher degrees, but the perfect type is best kept in view by the use of the qualified form expressed by the adjective "spontaneous"—meaning voluntary, without reward, except as found in the act itself. This qualification is almost necessary to prevent the lowering of the value of the term, as "perfect" was required to express Christ-Love, in contradistinction to worldly love.

OPTIMISM

Optimism is *forethought.* Christianity, pure and undefiled, is perfect optimism. Christ is the Perfect Optimist.[*]

FORETHOUGHT

"Forethought" is *the logical, trustful, hopeful, Christian, and therefore stimulating, consideration of the future.*

Forethought cannot be contrasted as the opposite of fearthought for the same reason that a tree cannot be contrasted as the opposite of its shadow; one being the growing, fruit-bearing substance; and the other being the unsubstantial, unillumined simulation of the living reality.

ENVIRONMENT

Surroundings which impress themselves upon the mind and assist to influence and form character and opinions.

SPIRITUAL CEREBRATION

Sometimes called unconscious cerebration; *intelligence not derived*

---

[*] Note: The motto of Optimism is, as elsewhere stated, "*All can be,* and therefore *shall be,* well."

from experience; principally obtained during undisturbed sleep, and, seemingly, supernaturally clear to consciousness on awakening in natural manner; Spiritual Cerebration is man's best partner, if confidently listened to, heeded and followed.

NATURAL SELECTION

Unconscious physical attraction; assisting sustenance, protection, development and reproduction; attribute of all life.

DIVINE SELECTION

Attribute only of Man; distinguishing Man from the rest of Creation; exercised in modifying the brute law of the "survival of the fittest, or strongest," by cultivating harmonic conditions favoring growth and producing happiness; God's Higher Law of Harmony executed through Man.

HAPPINESS

The evidence and fruit and reward of growth as involved in Altruism.

NATURE

As commonly used, "nature" means creation apart from man. The accepted definition is "creation," and as such includes man and all created things, and also the processes of creation—generation, degeneration and regeneration—as involved in growth. The common use of the word "nature" is a convenient one, and hence let us make use of it as meaning *creation other than man.*

EGOCIATION

Egociation is, *Appreciation of self as a creation of God and as an instrument of Altruism*—to be cultivated to its greatest possibilities in order that it may render *Altruistic service in the execution of the Higher Law of Harmony.*

There are two distinct kinds of *ego*—self: The *ego* that is physically and intellectually born only, and whose tendencies are egotistically selfish, and therefore, *animalesque*: And the *ego* that enjoys Appreciation, realizes God, loves spontaneously, understands the Higher Law of Harmony and serves with enthusiasm in the execution of the Law by the exercise of Divine Selection, and thereby attains True Happiness.

The mental equipment of the unthinking is dulled by a confusion of these two *egos*, and hence they cultivate egotism, believing it to be *Egociation*; as they cultivate *fearthought*, believing it to be forethought; and as they tolerate license, believing it to be an attribute of liberty.

The desirability of separating the lower, or animal, self from the Higher Self, warrants the coining of a term, sufficiently new to attract attention and sufficiently allied to well-known words to explain itself. With this object in view I have empirically selected a combination of *ego* and *appreciation*, and in so doing, have coined the euphonious term *Egociation* as an antithesis of "egotism," especially useful in inculcating a general understanding of the Higher Law of Harmony and in securing recognition of the place of the Higher Self within the Law.

In the cultivation of Egociation, man recognizes and asserts an *individuality*, or *responsibility*, as a part of the whole, the result of appreciation, opposed to *personality* or *separateness*, which is an attribute of egotism.

Words that carry good suggestion with them are less liable to do harm by being variously understood than those that convey bad suggestion. These latter should be defined in such a manner as to clearly suggest their badness; in fact, war should be waged upon them by every possible means.

EGOTISM

"Egotism" is *separation from God*. The fruit of egotism is selfishness.

SELFISHNESS

In the list of the deterrents, selfishness holds bottom place. Self-forethought, self-carefulness, self-culture, and self-respect, are in no way related to selfishness, but are provision of strength towards useful purposes. Selfishness is the mark of animal origin. We will therefore define it as *relic of animalism remaining in man*.

Selfishness is the opposite of altruism. While a suggestion of altruism is found in some animals, especially in dogs, it is not an animal characteristic. Selfishness is the predominant animal trait and therefore excuses the otherwise unkindly comparison.

FEAR

Fear is also a relic of animalism, and a child of selfishness—a deformed child of an ill-formed parent. It is not a physical condition, but simply an expression of fearthought. We will therefore define "fear" as *an expression of fearthought*.

FEARTHOUGHT

"Fearthought" is *the self-imposed or self-permitted suggestion of inferiority*. It is both a *cause* and an *effect* of selfishness. It is the "tap-root of evil."

"Fearthought" was coined by the author in order, if possible by suggestion, to separate from divinely ordained forethought any element of apprehension or weakness that might be masquerading under the name of forethought in the minds of the unthinking.

WORRY

"Worry" is fearthought in contradistinction to forethought.

ANGER

"Anger" is *the brutal and self-inflicting expression of disapproval—*brutal, because it is ungodly, unchristian and unaltruistic; *self-inflicting*, because the ill-effect of it reacts upon the person enangered.

There can be no "righteous anger." Disapproval there must be, because man has been endowed with the faculty of *Divine Selection*, and thereby shows a divinity denied to all other living things whose preferences are called in Science "natural selection." Disapproval in the interest of harmony—*Divine Selection*—and disapproval in the creation of discord—anger—are, the one holy, and the other unholy, uses of the faculty of selection.

There may be, then, *righteous disapproval*, but there never can be "righteous anger."

ENVY

"Envy" is anger of non-possession. "Envy" is sometimes wrongly used to express appreciation, as, "I envy you your good fortune," but we will give it the one meaning of "anger of non-possession."

JEALOUSY

"Jealousy" is "the homage that inferiority pays to merit";* or, *recognition or confession of inferiority*; or, *fearthought*.

---

* Note—I take this apt definition of "jealousy" from that excellent periodical—the organ of the League of American Wheelmen—"The Bulletin and Good Roads." Many good suggestions in menticulture accompany the excellent suggestions relative to good roads in this paper. Good thoughts are good roads to good action.

TAP-ROOT

"Tap-root" is "the chief root." It is the main support of the tree, of nearly the size of the trunk, and without which the tree must fall and die. The tap-root strikes deep into the soil, while the surface-roots reach out along the surface. For example; egotism is the tree of evil, either selfishness or fearthought is the tap-root, and anger and worry in all their phases are the surface roots of the tree. The tree is known by its fruits, which are, separation, paralysis, disease, unhappiness and death.

TROUBLE

Trouble does not really exist. Fearthought of trouble is as near as one ever gets to the condition, for the reason that whatever has come has already ceased to exist, except in the memory. The reason for so fine a distinction is made clear under the caption of "The Impotence of Pain," and is emphasized in order to place merited responsibility on fearthought. What is called "trouble," however, can be defined as *unwelcome conditions*, but, if analyzed, the chief elements of the "conditions" will be found to be *fearthought of still more unwelcome conditions*. The tap-root, then, of trouble is fearthought.

PESSIMISM

Pessimism is *fearthought*. Pessimism is the devil.

NERVOUSNESS

Nervousness is generally an *effect* and not a *cause*. It is the immediate or reflex result of fearthought.

TEMPERAMENT

Like "nervousness," so-called, "temperament"—habit-of-feeling—is generally an effect and not a cause; and is frequently used as an excuse for self-indulged weaknesses.

The value of simile.

CHRIST TAUGHT ALMOST ENTIRELY by parable.

Apropos of the value of simile is an experiment about which I have recently heard.

An experimenter wished to measure in some way the strength of certain vibrations and their effect upon vibratory things. A large steel comb, such as is used in music-boxes to produce sounds, was constructed. Each tooth was made as nearly as possible just like every other tooth. They not only seemed to measure alike, but when set in motion the vibrations seemed to be alike to the sense of hearing.

There was also constructed a huge tuning-fork, large enough to be struck with a bar of iron, and whose vibrations, when it was struck, came forth in big undulating waves like the pealing of a temple bell.

The object of the experiment was to observe, through the effect of powerful vibrations on the teeth of the resonant comb, a possible difference, too slight to be measured by calipers or by striking the teeth separately. The sound-waves, coming alike to all, would affect all alike unless there should be a difference in the receptivity of the teeth owing to differing density of metal, size, or some other condition not measurable by other means. By listening attentively near to the comb, the effect of the vibrations on the separate teeth could be heard.

The tuning-fork was placed about forty feet away from the steel comb, and was struck a heavy blow with the iron bar. Only three of the twelve teeth vibrated in response. The others were not in sympathy. *They did not hear the sound.*

I did not see the experiment, but it will serve to illustrate the value of simile.

All knowledge is measured by comparison. The most effective teaching is done through parable or simile. A so-called magnetic orator or writer reaches his hearers or readers by aid of apt simile. In this the orator has the advantage. If one simile does not convey the point he wishes to make, he tries another and yet another until he has detected sympathetic signs of approval in the majority of his audience. If there are present a hundred listeners, it may require ten stories or ten similes to reach the entire hundred, as there may be ten kinds of interest or sympathy present to be reached. Farmers and gardeners may not be familiar with the terms that describe the experience of the mariner; mechanics may not understand the language of the counting room or of the various exchanges; and men may not appreciate the special accomplishments, sympathies, weaknesses or foibles of women. Each individual is a separate tooth or string in the instrument called society. Heredity and environment have tempered and shaped each individual differently from his fellows. Truth is always the same, but the vibrations that carry it must be regulated to suit the conditions and understandings of each person, or group of persons, to be harmonized by it.

In an attack upon offensive and evil things, offensive similes are best employed. It is an application of the principle that a thief can best catch a thief. The object of this little book is to wage war upon fearthought and its brood of evil children. This is the excuse for writing under such offensive captions as "Don't Be a Sewer," and "Thou Shalt Not Strike a Woman," and also such ungrammatical caption as "I Can't *Not* Do It."

It is the opinion of the author that we are in the habit of taking evil too seriously. Evil is usually ridiculous, and while it thrives under the stimulation of serious consideration, it cannot stand ridicule. Shrewd politicians know this, and hence depend more upon the political cartoon to kill the political enemy, than upon all the reading matter possible to be printed.

What the terms "God," "Appreciation," "Mother," "Love," "Altruism," "Egociation," "Forethought," "Happiness," etc., stand for, should be reverenced and glorified; while the devil, egotism, selfishness, fearthought, anger and worry, and all of their various expressions, should be ridiculed out of respectability.

There is no intent to make vulgar excuses for the method of presentation of the simple and aged truths which are the subject of the present book. For the same reason that I have asked my readers to agree with me as to the meaning of terms in connection with the discussion, I ask them to allow me to state my reasons for the method of the presentation, if it should seem unusual and, perhaps, undignified.

Analysis of Fear.

PROFESSOR ANGELO MOSSO, the eminent physiologist of Turin, Italy, who has experimented with the condition and results of fear to a greater extent than any one else that I know of, has published a volume entitled "Fear."*

Professor Mosso writes of much regarding fear that we can all corroborate from personal experience as to the uncomfortableness of the emotion, and also informs us of much that is instructive as to the baleful effects of the mischief it produces upon the tissues of the body. He states that, unconsciously or consciously, the effect of fear is found to be disarrangement, which allows or causes inflammation, fever and other unhealthy conditions that are favorable to the nesting of the microbes of special diseases, such as are sometimes found in the air or in the water that we take in, and which are ever waiting for a chance to nest and breed.

An eminent English physician has also communicated to a leading English magazine a belief that fear directly attacks the individual molecules of the body and causes a disarrangement, a relaxing, a letting-go condition of the molecules in their relation to

---

* Messrs. E. Lough and F. Kiesow, pupils of Professor Mosso, translated the fifth Italian edition of "Fear" into English, and Longmans, Green and Company published it in 1896.

adjoining molecules, and that the relaxed condition is that in which disease originates. He states that there are means of communication within the body that are as direct and distinct as are the wires that convey the electric fluid from point to point, and that they connect the brain or nervous centers with each pair of molecules. By these means the sense of fear travels, weak or strong, in response to every pulse of its activity.

Within our visible experience, we know how completely the emotion of fear, or any of its various expressions can upset the stomach, suspend the appetite and even cause instant death. So evident are the bad effects of fear, that it is necessary only to refer to them before suggesting a remedy; but there are some powerful illustrations that are interesting, and which will be found under the caption of "Baleful Effects of Fear."

In this connection, what we are most interested in is, how to rid ourselves of the habit of fear. Fear is not a physical thing. It is the result of fearthought, and, being fearthought, has no more substance than other thought.

In animals it is an attribute of instinct, and is a wise provision of protection. In the human young, it is not so. In the helplessness of human fœtal existence and infancy, we find a perfectly clean, but wonderfully impressionable, thought-matrix, into which are to be impressed the suggestions whose sum constitutes the intelligence in men which takes the place of instinct in animals.

Fear is no constituent part of the composition of this thought-matrix. Susceptibility to fearthought, as it is susceptible to any and all suggestions, is the nearest approach to inherent infliction of fear that the unfolding soul is burdened with. If the race-habit-of-thought were indelibly pock-marked by fear, and stamped its roughness on the thought-matrix of all mankind, there would be no one free from it; but, as many are born into, and live, a life of great strength and courage, free from any taint of fearthought, this assumption is disproved, and is as absurd as would be the assumption that man must always do whatever, and only what, his ancestors did.

All of the fear-impressions received are the result of either prenatal or post-natal suggestion. It is within the power of parents and nurses to keep the delicate susceptibility of their charges free from the curse of fearthought; or to cause or allow it to be scared and bruised by the claws of the demon.

President G. Stanley Hall, of Clarke University, Editor in Chief of the *American Journal of Psychology*, and Dr. Colin A. Scott, Professor of Psychology and Child Study at the Cook County Normal School, Chicago, Ill., U. S. A., have rendered greatest service to humanity by searching out and analyzing fears in children, exposing the absurdity of them, showing the sources from which foolish fears are derived, and thereby dragging from ambush the worst enemy of mankind, whose strength is developed by means of secret toleration, but can easily be overcome if uncovered.

The method of securing information was by means of the *questionaire*, the answers to which, although unsigned and unidentifiable, and savoring of exaggeration or romance, furnish splendid texts in a crusade against the toleration of the habit-of-fear in a civilized community. One can scarcely imagine, before reading the answers to the fear *questionaire*, the unreasonable and absurd fears that warp the lives and ruin the health of many of the people among whom we move, and by whom, in some measure, we and our children are unconsciously influenced.

If it were the community-habit-of-thought that fear was an unnecessary thing and an evil thing, and not respectable and not Christian, many of these fears would not exist, owing to the proneness of all persons to imitation and their acceptance of community-of-habit-thought as law and gospel. Fear is a very insidious thing. It will enter the smallest opening, and ferment, and increase, and permeate whatever it attacks, if it be permitted foothold in the least degree.

We have too little time in life personally to investigate all of the causes of things that are pertinent to our living and working, or to learn the reason for their leading to observed results. We are indebted to Professor Mosso, Dr. Hall, Dr. Scott and other painstaking scientists, for observing the habits of our enemies, and for giving the results of their observations in such agreeable forms as are the intimate and frank analyses of fear given in Professor Mosso's book and other treatises on the subject; but what we are most interested in is, how to kill or how to escape fearthought within ourselves and, ultimately, how to protect our children against the evil.

To digress somewhat, and as an excuse for using the terms of parable and homely experience instead of the terms of science: It is said that the use of alum for the settling of impurities out of water was an old housewife's remedy for a very long time before any scientist studied the chemical change that effected the result.

The old housewives knew by experience, as well as did the doctors, that alum *would* "settle" water, but it was left to the latter to say *why* it did so. We are, therefore, mainly indebted to a chance discovery, and to the preservation of the formula by housewives, for our ability to purify water by means of alum.

In the same manner we have discovered, perhaps by accident, that certain suggestions will purify our minds, by eliminating special fears by which we have been dominated. We also have learned by experiment that all fear is eliminable by use of sufficiently powerful suggestion made to fit the particular fear experimented against. I *know that the deterrent passions can be eradicated*; and, *easier than not.* Others *know* this also, and are living lives of beautiful strength, freedom and happiness, who once were slaves to fearthought; and many such there already are, and their number is increasing very rapidly under the influence of the observation of unfailing, profitable results in consequence.

If we *know* that anything *can be done*, it is not vitally essential that we should know *why* it is possible.

Experience, in conveying the suggestion, has taught that there is *some* way to reach, and to dispel, any special fear.

Science will some time, undoubtedly, be able to tell us just how to treat each form of fear in a scientific manner, but in the meantime we *know* that it is possible to cure all of the separate forms of fear by rooting out the basic fear—the fear of death—and by conveying the all-powerful suggestion that all fear is needless and unprofitable.

Baleful effects of Fear.

IN THE LAST chapter I stated that the bad effects of fear were so well known to every one that it was not necessary to dwell upon them, but second thought suggests stating a few special cases that have been told me by physician friends who are interested in the lay experiments I am making.

In the Southern States of the United States of America, where the black race comes into closest touch with Caucasian civilization under conditions of free expression, is probably the best place to study fear and its opposite, chivalrous courage.

Dr. William E. Parker, of the Charity Hospital of New Orleans, was once called to attend a big negro who had been brought in by the ambulance, and whom the students in charge of the ambulance had frightened nearly to death by telling that he was badly wounded in the stomach, and would probably die.

The negro was big and burly and black, and yet, livid with fear. Both pulse and temperature indicated serious trouble within, and the convulsive tremors that shook him from time to time revealed a state of collapse that might end in death at any time. There was no outward flow of blood, but the probable inward flow seemed more dangerous in consequence.

The account of the case, as related by the students, told of a shooting affray, in which the negro had been hit in the abdomen, as evidenced by a bullet-hole in his clothing.

Dr. Parker began an examination by ordering the clothing of the patient removed, and during which a bullet, much flattened, fell upon the floor. This bullet had done no serious injury, of course, but there might have been two shots and two bullets, one of which had penetrated the body, and hence the bullet that fell upon the floor caused no special attention, till search had been made in vain for a hole in the skin. Complete examination revealed the fact that the negro had been hit, but that the bullet had struck a button, causing a bruised place behind the button, but had lodged in the clothing, in harmless inertia.

As the doctor held up the bullet, and told the patient of the slight extent of his injury and the wonder of his escape, good, warm blood returned to the livid countenance, the pulse and the temperature assumed their normal condition, a grateful sparkle lit up the almost glassy eyeballs, and the broadest possible grin spread over the face of the erstwhile dying man.

The negro got down from the operating-table, arranged his clothing, and, after apologizing for the trouble he had caused, and after thanking the doctor and the students for their attentions, went out into the street as well as ever. He had been, half an hour before, at death's door.

Dr. Henry A. Veazie, one of the student-heroes of the yellow-fever epidemic of 1878, who had splendid opportunity to witness the effects of fear during an epidemic, asserts that fear is a certain cause of attack of yellow fever.

I will say, parenthetically, in the way of right information relative to the South, that there has been no epidemic since 1878—twenty years; that it has been proven that yellow fever does not originate in any part of the United States, and that it is very effectively barred out at quarantine, or, if accidentally admitted, that it is easily killed by present means of treatment, and that an epidemic is no longer mentioned as a possibility—only as quite a remote memory—in New Orleans, or elsewhere in the South.

Doctor Veazie's story is corroborated by an able brochure on

"The Influence of Fear in Disease," by the much-beloved, the late Dr. William H. Holcomb, of New Orleans; and, so helpful are the suggestions contained in it, that I have secured the privilege from the Purdy Publishing Company, of Chicago, of reprinting largely from it, and have added the matter copied as "Appendix A," to this volume.[*]

Doctor Veazie also called my attention to the unusual fatality attending what are called "frog-accidents." Train-handlers and yardmen employed on railroads are very liable to these "frog-accidents." The frog is that part of a switch where the rails come together, forming a "V." In running about recklessly, as a train-man generally does, he sometimes catches the sole of a boot in the "V," and wedges it in so tightly that the foot cannot be withdrawn. If a locomotive, or a car, happen to be coming towards him, and cannot be stopped in time, cutting off of the foot or the leg by the wheels upon the rails is a certain result.

If it were done instantly, and without a foreknowledge of the owner of the leg or foot, the chances of recovery would be almost assured, because of the present skill of surgery and the efficacy of known antiseptics; but with the few moments of foreknowledge of the impending accident, the poison of fearthought has time to so unnerve the system, relax the tissues, and itself disease the body by shock, that the wounding usually results in death.

There is probably no situation in which a person can be placed where the conditions are more horrible than to be wedged between the rails, and to see an eighty-ton locomotive rolling on to him with irresistible weight. Being condemned to be hanged cannot be as fearful, for the reason that the condemned has been led gradually to contemplate the possibility of death by this means, and has come to expect it with a certain amount of complacency. The terror of the "frog-accident" comes with the suddenness of its possibility and the helplessness of the situation. It is like an ice-water bath thrown on a sweating person. It is the icy hand of death come to clutch at the

---

[*] Two other brochures by Dr. Holcomb are published by the Purdy Company. They are "Condensed Thoughts about Christian Science" and "The Power of Thought in the Production and Cure of Disease."

throat of warmest hope and fondest affections. As such, it must be fearful; but, to the person habituated to *fear* fear, through knowing the deadly effect of it, the emotion can be prepared for, greatly modified and possibly counteracted, by a prearrangement with the emotional self—that which Hudson calls the "subjective mind."

To be effective in case of surprise, the preparation must come from the habit-of-feeling, "*I must not be afraid; I must not be afraid.*" No matter what the surprise, the emotional self must instantly assert, through habit, "*I must not be afraid.*"

I have not had experience with "frog-accidents" to test the efficacy of my theory of schooled suggestion, but I have been subject to surprises that have been quite as fearful. As it happened, the incident I speak of was not perilous, but it had all the appearance of being so to me, when I was awakened from sleep, in a hotel in New York City, by suffocation, to find my room full of smoke that poured in through the transom and through the cracks of the door which was my only means of escape.

My room was on the fifth floor of the hotel, and the house had the reputation of being a "fire-trap."

As soon as my reasoning-self had time to take in the situation, the probability of being burned to death seemed almost certain; but before that happened—that is, before the reasoning-self had analyzed the situation—the habit-of-thought self had asserted many times, and constantly, "You *must not be afraid! you must not be afraid*"; and, as a result, I was *not afraid*; and the calm of the moment allowed me to measure chances and arrange expedients, as if there were no danger imminent.

It was a case of much smoke and little fire, but there were those in the hotel who were made very ill by the fright of it.

If I had always been free from the emotion of fear, and had not been a sorry victim to it in some special forms, "natural temperament" could be urged as a cause of the calm I enjoyed during the incident related above; but such is not the case. I have been subjected to shocks of various kinds, incident to an adventurous life, that have been powerful impressions for evil upon my emotional self, and it is personal experience of cure and relief that I am giving in support of my theory.

The experience of Mr. George Kennan, the Siberian traveler, and brilliant writer and lecturer, relative to fear and its cure, is singularly like my own, and was related to me in an exchange of personal confidences, last year.

The *Atlantic Monthly* for May, 1897, contains an excellent account of Mr. Kennan's case, and I am permitted by the publishers, Messrs. Houghton, Mifflin & Company, to reprint it; which I have done under Appendix "B."

Fear is rarely general as related to different causes for fearthought. I have been told of a case of specific fear that is interesting because of its unreasonableness. It was the case of a filibuster who had been on several raids where death was the almost certain penalty for being caught, and where the chances of being caught were almost certain. On the frontier our subject was known as a dare-devil, not afraid of anything, and yet he was always in mortal terror of a dark room. In infancy he had been scared into obedience by tales of goblins in the dark, and he had never rid himself of their influence. Anything on earth he could see held no terror for him, but he could not see the phantoms he created in the dark, and was therefore a slave to fear of them. It is probable that the bravado of his active life was partly caused by the desire to "average up" on courage, and, if so, the baleful effects of fear in this case were very far-reaching and destructive to the peace of society.

General experience teaches that whenever you find a bully, you find a yellow streak of cowardice somewhere in his composition; and, more than probable, bravado is assumed by him, in order to "square" himself with his own self-respect.

How to eliminate Fear.

IT HAS BEEN OBSERVED that the rooting out of any particular phase of fearthought, weakens the strength of all of the other phases. For instance, suppression of *anger* and *worry* tends to suppress all suspicion, and even fear itself, while special attack upon the fearthought called envy will perceptibly diminish the tendency to jealousy and avarice. There seems to be such close relationship between all of the forms of fearthought, that whatever affects one, affects all.

Fear of death undoubtedly underlies all fearthought. Fear of poverty, fear of accident, fear of sickness, all reach further than these calamities, to the possibility of death resulting from them. In this way we can trace all expressions of fear, either directly or indirectly, through the different forms of selfness, to fearthought of death.

In *Menticulture* I suggested the elimination of *anger* and *worry* as the roots of all the evil passions. On page 17, however, I gave "fear" as the tap-root of the evil emotions, including anger and worry, and stated my reason for attacking the surface roots best known and associated together, rather than the tap-root itself. It was because I believed at the time *Menticulture* was written, with people in general, that fear was a constituent weakness of all consciousness, and only expressions of it were eliminable.

I find in my later experience in practice, however, and in

conveying the suggestion to others, that fear itself is possible to be rooted out by the force of counter-suggestion of one sort or another, and that there is no mental habit or impression that cannot be counteracted by some other more powerful habit or impression, and that it is best to attack the bottom cause of all weaknesses at once, and thereby wage warfare upon their innermost citadel.

As fearthought is the parent of all the evil emotions, so is fear of death the first of all the causes of fearthought.

It is not a difficult matter to eliminate the fear of death. It is first necessary to do away with any dread of a lifeless human body. There are few who feel dread of the flesh of animals as they see it hanging in the stalls of the butchers. There is no more reason to have a feeling of fear in connection with the sight of dead human flesh than there is to feel uncomfortable in the presence of the flesh of a lifeless lamb or a lifeless chicken.

There have lived people who were as accustomed to seeing human flesh exposed in butchers' shops as we are accustomed to see the flesh of animals so exposed, and there is an engraving of a cannibal meat-stall in Huxley's "Man's Place in Nature," copied from an old book of travel to the coast of Africa, which Mr. Huxley offers authoritatively.

The subject may seem to be a grewsome one to many readers, and reference to the customs of cannibals may shock their supersensitive habits of thought, but the object is sufficient justification. Such may, however, soothe their injured feelings by remembering that our meat-selling and meat-eating customs seem as inhuman to many Buddhists as do the customs of cannibals to us.

If we value essentials impartially, soul and mind count above everything, and tissue which they once animated counts for nothing when they have left it, no matter what have been the associations, especially if dread of the dead tissue inspires emotions that are detrimental to the welfare of soul or mind.

My object in suggesting a systematic reversal of our feeling towards lifeless human flesh is because it is a basic cause of fear. Remove this dread, and half of the terror of death is removed with it.

In this connection, the suggestion should be urged, that separation—as in death—is unessential as compared with the privilege of having known a beloved one, and that appreciation and gratitude should always outweigh regret in relation to an inevitable change.

All of the observed processes of nature teach that every normal change is for the better, and the change called death is as normal as the change called birth. The full term of human life is but a pin-point in the great span of evolution. How unreasonable it is to protest the measurement of the breadth of a pin-point with Him who doeth all things well!

Life is like the ticking of a clock; each passing of the pendulum may be a day or a year; when the clock strikes, one period only is ended, but a new period is also begun. Why mourn at the striking of the clock! A new and happier hour has begun. Why mourn the passing on of a beloved one! For to Christian, or to Buddhist, as well as to all sentient beings, a new and a better life has then begun.

The attitude towards the separation called death should be such as to induce the thought, and even the expression, "Pass on, beloved; enter into the better state which all of the processes of nature teach are the result of every change; it will soon be my time to follow; my happiness at your preferment attend you; my love is blessed with that happiness; and what you have been to me remains, and will remain forever. Amen."

Sorrow was dignified by Christ. He has been wrongfully called "The Man of Sorrow." His sorrow was for the evils which men suffered, and never was caused by any of the beneficent decrees of the Father. Protest against the decrees of the Father is blasphemy. Some forms of sorrow are blasphemy.

Sorrow and optimism do not go together. Christ was (and is) the Supreme Optimist, and taught nothing but optimism. Tears do not always express sorrow. Wherein tears express selfishness, especially in the form of anger, they are bad. Wherein tears are free from selfishness, they may do no great harm. In such case, what may seem to be sorrow may be an expression of loving sympathy, and, as such, may be good.

Without careful analysis of the quality of the emotion, love may be thought to be righteous cause for fearthought. This is a vicious thought. Nothing is righteous that is harmful, and fearthought is harmful. Love, without any element of fearthought in it, is infinitely better than love that is tinctured with fearthought. Forethought is the necessary accompaniment of perfect love, but fearthought is its enemy.

Separation can be made to gladden love through self-sacrifice. Separation—as in death—can be made to gladden love by supreme self-sacrifice to the beloved one who is preferred by death, and thereby made to disarm that underlying fear of all fears—the fear of death.

If, however, the fear of lifeless human flesh is eliminated, the fear of death itself will be found to be greatly modified. From this point the elimination of special pet fears, whether of the individual or of the community sort, will become an easy matter, as the greater is but the sum of the lesser.

In looking for means with which to attack so great an enemy as fear, either in one's self or in another, any weapon is a good weapon that is found to be effective. Logic is more respectable, but such is the foolishness of many forms of fear that ridicule is more often effective. Appeal to honor, self-respect, love, logic, ridicule, and to *fear itself*, may be had in so worthy a cause as the vanquishing of the arch-enemy of growth and happiness.

Old soldiers sometimes admit that their courage in battle has been the result of their fear of seeming to be cowards. When the far-reaching and poisonous effect of the evil of fearthought is properly understood, and the possibility of its elimination generally believed in, people will be *afraid* to be afraid—afraid of ridicule and criticism, as well as afraid of evil and unhealthful effects. The cure will have been homœopathic, in that like has been employed to cure (or kill) like.

Logic is the most rational weapon, but ridicule is sharper. Logic may not cure a robust woman of the woman-habit-of-thought that a mouse is a fearsome thing, but reference to the fact that it is ridiculous for a five-foot woman to be afraid of a two-inch mouse may effect the result, especially when it is known that the mouse is more afraid of the woman, according to his capacity for fear, than it is possible for the woman to be afraid of the mouse.

Acquaintance is another effective cure. It may not be necessary that all afflicted ones should serve an apprenticeship at undertaking in order to be cured of fear of a lifeless human body, but if the fear of a corpse cannot be eradicated by other means, it is worth while to do that or *anything else*, no matter how uncanny or disagreeable, in order to accomplish the object. So necessary is the eradication of the germ principle of fear to the cultivation of growth and happiness, that if it is found that fear of the lifeless human body cannot be cured otherwise, even a real apprenticeship in a hospital dissecting-room would be a profitable expedient as a last resort. To seek the acquaintance of fearsome insects and animals, through close observation and study of their habits, is better than to suffer harm from a needless prejudice against them.

Cure of the fear of one dreaded insect or reptile is sure to modify the fear of all other things dreaded, so that the difficult part of the cure is acquiring the belief that it is possible, and making the resolve to attempt it.

If parents realized the full importance of the eradication of fearthought from the minds of their children, they would stop immediately all other occupation, and rest not nor be content until the germ of fearthought in their children had been located and killed; and those skilled in such search and cure would become the physicians most in demand.

How to cure special forms of Fear.

EXCITING INTEREST in the intrinsic beauties and usefulness of things thought to be disagreeable or dreadful, is an excellent way of curing fear of them.

I once had an opportunity of experimenting with this method of curing particular fears by testing it on a mother and children whose *bête noire* was a thunderstorm.

I had seen them at the World's Columbian Exposition, wrapt in the enjoyment of the great displays of fireworks that were operated on the lake front of the Exposition grounds each evening. I also happened to be provided with statistics, showing that the chance of being struck by lightning was only one in a great many thousand, and that if one were to seek to be struck, he would have to wait about ten thousand years for his average turn. I recalled the greater real beauty of the natural fireworks of the summer season, and their comparative harmlessness. This was the logic of it, and modified somewhat the attitude of the children, as well as the fear of the mother, relative to lightning and thunder; but the real cure came through appreciative suggestion and acquaintance.

On the approach of a storm wherein lightning might be expected, and even before it was visible, the mother had been in the habit of assuming a frightened expression, of gathering the children together, of cowering in a corner, and sometimes in a closet, in fear and trembling, until the storm had passed. From infancy the children had been in the habit of associating something fearful with the idea of lightning and thunder, and had never had a chance to observe their beauties.

I started in to correct the bad impressions, and to teach the attractiveness of storm phenomena, by calling out, on the approach of a storm, somewhat in this wise: "Oh! children, do you remember the beautiful fireworks at the Exposition? Come here quick! let's watch; we are going to have something ten times more beautiful, and, oh! such big booms and bangs. Watch now! ah! that wasn't much, but keep a-watching and we'll have some beauties. Crash! bang! blizzard! My! but wasn't that a beauty? Watch sharp, now, or you'll miss the best one,—what! afraid? Why, Alice, afraid of a beautiful thing like that! Nonsense! Come here, dear, and sit in my lap and watch out sharp, and then you *can't* be afraid. There! that's a little lady. Splendid! I reckon you know how to enjoy something beautiful, as well as any one. Boom, boom, boom! Did you ever hear anything so grand? Great big drums up yonder. I wonder what sort of a Fourth of July they are having? Wouldn't World's-Fair fireworks seem tame beside this? And think of it!—they don't cost a cent, and they are clearing the atmosphere so that the sun will shine brighter to-morrow than it ever did. It will shine for us, and for the plants, and for the butterflies. My! but aren't we lucky to have good eyes and good ears when such things are going on! and don't we pity the poor little blind and deaf children! Does lightning sometimes strike people and kill them? Why, yes, once in a great, great long while; but when it does, they say it is the pleasantest sensation possible. Don't you mind when you have pleasant shivers, what a delightful feeling it is? Well, they say being struck by lightning is like that—only more so. I have never had the experience of being killed by lightning, of course, but when my turn to enter the next life comes, I hope it will be that way; but the chances of being that lucky are very slim. Somebody, some great schoolmaster that knows almost everything, has calculated that if a man wanted to be struck by lightning he would probably have to wait about ten thousand years. That is too long. Life is delightful as it is; but if I had to wait even a thousand years or even an hundred years more for my promotion that way, I think I would rather choose a more common and less agreeable way"; and so on, governed by the interest and the effect upon the children. I impressed on them the real beauty of the storm, and taught them appreciation, to take the place of fear.

It is needless to say that that family no longer dreads the storm cloud. The suggestion reversed their way of looking at storms, and they then found great beauty in them and ceased to fear them.

Another experience: I once had the privilege of spending some time in close relations of friendship to a family composed of a widowed mother and several children, sons, daughter, nephews and nieces. A sister of the mother, who was pronounced to be an incurable invalid, had come from her Northern home to seek relief in the climate of the Southland. It is impossible to imagine more tender care of an invalid. Each member of the family vied with the others in offering gentle attentions, so that the waning life was filled with happiness that made invalidism almost a pleasure, as being the cause of so much loving consideration.

One morning the life-light flickered for a little and then went out. The usual funeral preparations which are the custom were attended to, and the remains were sent away to the far-distant home, and the family burial-lot.

While the remains were awaiting the appointed time of removal, the children of the family, of all ages and both sexes, passed in and out of the death-chamber, by day or by night, as if there had been no death, and there was not a semblance of dread, nor fearthought nor mourning. It was such a beautiful expression of loving consideration, unmarred by dread or fearthought, that one might well choose such a time and such a place and such environment on the occasion of one's passing on to the better life.

If it be possible to be a spirit, conscious of material environment, and in such guise to attend one's own funeral, which would be the environment of choice? Egotism, disembodied, would undoubtedly choose a scene of violent mourning, long drawn out, and painful to as many as possible. Loving Unselfishness would as certainly choose a funeral scene such as I witnessed in the house of my friends. Which would you choose? And if, as is most reasonable to suppose from observing the sequences of nature's processes that show that the seed of a flower has a more nearly perfect flower enfolded within itself, spirits also become purer by each unfolding through the release called death, and being made pure and unegotistic by the change, they must prefer, if they have the privilege, to have their old home remains viewed with loving and fearless consideration, rather than with fearsome dread and ostentatious emotion.

Then let us abjure fear in connection with death, and also in connection with the mortal remains of the beloved.

If the conventional premises relative to death be correct, the common attitude towards it is useless; and if the hypothetical premises be correct, as it is better to suppose, even if we cannot assert it, the common attitude is worse than useless, for it is both harmful and unjust. If we cultivate fear and mourning in connection with death, we are unjust to the dead, we are unjust to the living, we are unjust to ourselves; and, above all, cruel to the tender and impressionable emotions of children, to whom we are constantly leaving legacies of cowardice and ignorant egotism, or legacies of pure suggestion, love and appreciation.

Much might be written about the subject of this chapter, and many illustrations could be given wherein illogical fears have been, or can be, ridiculed away, but inasmuch as some of the following chapters are mainly devoted to this purpose, it is not necessary to more than suggest a line of argument under the present caption.

The now-field.

LET us work together for a season in the Now-Field.

We cannot work in any other field, but we can and do waste much valuable time in trying to work in the past or in the future, and in so doing neglect the precious now.

For recreation we may pleasantly, and perhaps profitably, speculate as to what there may be in the way of atoms finer than star-dust, and as to the possible degree of invisibleness of the ultimate ether. We may also exercise and strengthen our imagination by trying to give form to the Source of it all. Tiring of guessing in these directions, we may vary our recreation by attempts to peep under or through the veil which Nature so persistently holds between the present conscious life and the one we hope for beyond the veil. It can do no harm to think form into a forgotten past and into an uncertain future, if, in so doing, the vital and superprecious now be well guarded against the things we know to be deterrent to the best growth of the life-plant.

In considering the duty of the now, let us, for convenience of comparison, liken life to an agricultural season of one year's duration. We find, in ourselves, that the seed from which we have unfolded has already been sown, and the life-plant pretty well grown before we attain consciousness of duty and begin to think independently. If we are lucky, we have been taught early what the

real object of life is, our duties in it, and the true values to be cultivated in connection with it.

We have very sensibly learned to get in out of the wet when it
rains, and many other useful aids to comfort as well as to protection,
but the most vital assistants of growth have been neglected, and
many positive deterrents to growth have been cultivated by those
who have been our teachers, and hence it behooves us to look to our
habits of thought and of action in order to get rid of those which are
detrimental to our growth.

Of first importance is the care of the Now-Field.

We have already suggested, and it cannot be too often repeated,
that the condition favorable and necessary to growth is that of
harmony—an harmonious present is the living heir and parent of all
harmonies—that growth is the evident object of life, and that when
anything ceases to grow it begins to die—there is no growth except
in the present, and no cultivable field other than the Now-Field—
that harmony, through one's ability to always furnish the concordant note, one's self, is within the power of each, regardless of environment or physical conditions, if *only* present conditions and
environment are considered, and that growth is the certain result of
harmony; that our function relative to growth is only to keep deterrent influences out of the present; that, if we do this, Nature never
fails to develop better results from the unfolding of each succession.
We have learned that all of the deterrents we have been able to
discover and classify are phases of fearthought; that fearthought is
no creation of the present, but is sought in the future and nourished
on the life-blood of the present—an excrescent and altogether para-
sitic abnormality, unnecessary to the thing it feeds on.

We have discovered, in our search for deterrents, that, if encoun-
tered in the now, they are easily routed. We have also discovered that
the longest life is but a succession of nows. If so, how easy becomes
the problem: Work diligently in the Now-Field.

In arguing against the potency of anger and worry and other
expressions of fearthought, where the contention has been persisted
in that they were necessary evils, and amenable only to suppression,
not to elimination, I have invariably won my point when suddenly

asking the question, "Are you angry or worried at this moment?" by the admission of my opponent, "No; not at this moment, because my mind is occupied with something which has no element of worry or anger in it." The replies vary, of course, but are to the same effect. I immediately return with the question: "Is not all time but a succession of nows, and, if so, cannot all of the nows, as well as this one, be exempt from apprehension and irritation, by continuing to think of pleasanter and more hopeful and helpful things?"

Each succeeding now is easier of control than the preceding one from which it learns the habit-of-control, and, if the immanent now is guarded, all the nows that follow will take care of themselves.

As we have observed, we need not think of the growing if we are only diligent in keeping fearthought out of our minds. Nature will do abundant growing for us, and if we do not seek fearthought beyond the now, we will have nothing to keep out. *It is easier than not!*

Does it not seem *very* easy when one thinks reasonably about it? If we confine our efforts to the Now-Field, we leave our enemy out in the cold by the comfortable process of non-invitation. Therefore, let us work together for a season in the Now-Field.

FEARTHOUGHT.

FEAR IS FEARTHOUGHT ONLY.

Fear is caused by the *self-imposed* or *self-permitted* suggestion of *inferiority*.

Fear is not a physical thing, but it causes physical derangement.

Fearthought is *self-imposed*, and is therefore unnecessary.

Fearthought, being evil and unnecessary, is therefore *not-respectable*.

Fearthought is a habit which is altogether irrational and illogical.

Fearthought is a parasite which, in civilized man, is entirely abnormal.

FEARTHOUGHT CAN BE ELIMINATED FROM THE MIND.

Fearthought is the tap-root of all evil and trouble.

Anger and *worry* are expressions of fearthought.

All forms of worry are directly caused by fearthought.

Anger is directly or indirectly caused by fearthought.

All of the evil passions which group themselves under the class-names of anger and worry are therefore the result of fearthought.

Fearthought is the result of egotism. Egotism is the reverse, or, rather, perverse, of Egociation. It is caused by self-separation from Co-operative-Strength, from Universal-Good—from God.

Selfishness is the fruit and the evidence of egotism.

Fearthought is the first expression of selfishness.

FEARTHOUGHT IS, THEREFORE, THE TAP-ROOT OF EVIL AND CONSEQUENT UNHAPPINESS.

Forethought invites success.

Fearthought invites failure.

The future is the vital part of life—the dead past furnishing only food for reminiscence and experience.

Consideration of the future must partake of either forethought or fearthought—it cannot partake of both at the same time.

Fearthought is in no way related to forethought except as the shadow is related to the tree behind which it hides from the light—the light of right-thinking.

Forethought stimulates, aids, fosters, encourages, and insures success of honest aims—its child is growth.

Fearthought relaxes, hampers, strangles, and thereby retards growth, to the end of dwarfing, if not killing, it—its children are paralysis, disease, unhappiness and death.

Forethought is a producer.

FEARTHOUGHT IS A ROBBER.

Forethought is constructive.

Fearthought is destructive.

Forethought suggests the building of houses for shelter wherein there can be no fearthought about storms.

Fearthought fusses and worries over the possibility of not getting the shelter ready in time to protect against inclement weather, and thereby wastes the available energy, and delays the completion of the shelter.

Forethought calmly proceeds to perform a useful task without fearthought of the extent of it. It does all that it can do—it can do no more.

Fearthought wrings its hands, and wastes its time in saying, "How can I ever do it?"

There is no difficulty in determining between forethought and fearthought.

Whatever thought is constructive, is forethought.

WHATEVER THOUGHT IS DESTRUCTIVE OR WASTEFUL IS FEARTHOUGHT.

———

Fearthought is the devil.

Fearthought is the arch-enemy of man, whose influence can be traced in every form of calamity and unhappiness.

Fearthought is the cause of indecision, suspicion, apprehension, jealousy, envy, indifference, self-degradation and all other forms of weakness which separate the afflicted from the tide of success and happiness, and which condemn them to the whirling and restless eddy of isolation and non-progression.

Fearthought is blasphemy, because it gives the lie to the fixed promises of God, as evidenced by experience.

Fearthought is like carbonic-acid gas pumped into one's atmosphere. It causes mental, moral and spiritual asphyxiation, and sometimes death—death to energy, death to tissue and death to all growth.

FEARTHOUGHT IS A LIAR, AND THE FATHER OF LIES.

———

Quarantine against Fearthought first.

Fearthought is more contagious than any other disease.

Fearthought is the chief distributer and promoter of other contagious diseases.

Fearthought can be guarded against by anti-toxic means, just as smallpox and diphtheria can be guarded against.

The serum to be used against fearthought is intelligent, persistent right suggestion.

Fearthought can also be quarantined against, the same as other contagious diseases.

Society can quarantine against fearthought by refusing to tolerate it as a necessity of civilized life—by classing it as not-respectable, and by refusing to feed it with sympathy.

Quarantine against fearthought in the individual is an easy matter to any one who will learn that it is only evil and never good.

Fearthought should be kept "without the gates."

Forethought for others is the most intelligent altruism.

Forethought is the natural condition, but can exist only in the absence of fearthought.

Forethought growing out of disagreeable or disastrous experience is a useful and worthy fruit; but fearthought taken from the same experience adds to the evil.

If a child be guarded against fearthought, he will enjoy immunity from it during life—a life twice or thrice prolonged in consequence. Parents should note the responsibility.

The consensus of the experience of parents, of physicians, of biologists, and of everyone who has observed child-life, is that the premises and deductions here given are correct, but as yet there has been no systematic effort made to eliminate fearthought out of the atmosphere of children, as there has been to eliminate weeds, malaria, contagious diseases, and other evils. Society should unite for defense against, and the extermination of, *childhood's worst enemy*.

Fearthought is the most pregnant cause of disaster and death.

Whoever teaches fearthought to a child, by either legend or example, may be a murderer by so doing.

Whoever permits or nurses fearthought within himself, sows the seed of suicide.

Whoever robs a child of the freedom of mind with which nature prefers to endow it, whether it be through pre-natal suggestion or through suggestion given after birth, is more a thief than one who robs it of its patrimony of goods or lands.

Whoever teaches or permits a child to suffer fearthought may never know the end of the disturbance caused thereby. Lying, stealing, avarice, suicide and murder may lie within the wake of its influence.

If parents have wronged their children unwittingly, they may yet correct the infliction by right example and by right counter-suggestions, lovingly, patiently, persistently and religiously given until the evil has been eradicated.

FEARTHOUGHT IS THE SEED OF SUICIDE.

Freedom is a Birthright.

Civilized Society insures Freedom.

The author has had much experience within the past few years which teaches that fearthought itself, and tendency to fearthought, are bad habits of the mind, that can be entirely counteracted if so desired, and if the desire be accompanied by reasonable assistance on the part of the afflicted ones.

Fearthought is the last relic of animal suspicion to be located, analyzed and dispelled. When it is entirely killed; then, and only then, will man become free—free to grow, free to appreciate his divine inheritance and free to enjoy it as ordained. As in agriculture and in horticulture, so in menticulture, and its contingent, physiculture, will it be found that deterrents to perfect growth can be eradicated, and that if attention to the germ-eradication of the deterrents is intelligent and persistent,

God will surely develop perfect growth and the perfect fruit of happiness.

Freedom is easier than not.

Fearthought is the result of ignorance or perversity.

Fearthought which is perverse is criminal.

Fearing for others is criminal, because it not only depresses and weakens them, but because it robs them of some part of the strength that encouragement and hopeful thought would give them.

Parents who do not wish to poison the natural energy of their children by depression and weakness, should learn the effect of telepathic influence for good or for evil, and thereby know that all of the expressions of fearthought are rank poisons.

Parents hold the key to character.

Whenever parents allow or teach their children to have fearthought, they foster in them the temptation to lie and steal.

Crime lurks in fearthought.

Ignorance is *not* bliss.

Ignorance can no longer be accepted as an excuse for the toleration of fear.

Thought precedes every emotion and every act of life. It must have no element of fear in it, if it is to lead up and on.

Habit-of-thought asserts itself on all occasions. *Habit-of-feeling* is the truer description, for the reason that it is the emotional self and not the thought-self that first responds to surprise.

Habit-of-thought or habit-of-feeling can be trained to respond to surprise with "I *must not be* afraid," as easily as it is permitted to respond with the cowardly dictum, "I *am* afraid."

If one have the habit-of-fearthought in any form or degree, surprise may cause it to inspire rash action which may end in disaster. More lives are lost through jumping *into* danger under the impulse of fearthought, than are ever saved by it. Calm forethought is the better friend in a case of peril than quaking fearthought.

I must not be afraid!

Fearthought is a dissembler.

Fearthought is a very dangerous enemy, because it habitually masquerades in the garb of forethought.

Many earnest persons who desire to cultivate only the best thought, believe that fearthought is forethought, and invite and nurse it as such.

The lexicographers even, have failed to separate fearthought from forethought, and hence it does not appear in the dictionaries under its specific descriptive appellation.

Let fear be disguised no longer. It is a child of ignorant or perverse imagination. It is fear*thought* only. It is always irrational and illogical. It has no element of good nor of protection in it. Separated from forethought, fearthought causes only paralysis and death, and neither energizes nor saves life. It is the devil. It is the result of false premises or impressions, but can be counteracted by logical premises and right impressions.

Fearthought is a masquerader.

The timid are the most impressionable, and can be cured of fearthought by intelligent, persistent, counter-suggestion.

Impressibility is as powerful an aid to good or right suggestion as it is to bad or false suggestion. Differently used, an element of weakness becomes an element of strength. In a matter of mind-accomplishment no one need say "I can't," for mind is what it most earnestly wishes to be.

Limiting weaknesses there are, at present, but these are generally found in asylums. A crusade against fearthought would, within one generation, make asylums unnecessary.

Average intelligence can be cleared of fearthought. A crusade against fearthought would immeasurably raise the average of intelligence.

Let no one deprecate himself or his fellows as to his or their possibilities. The timid may become courageous; the weak may become strong; the sick may become well, and the unhappy may become happy, by the reversal of the attitude of their energy toward life's problems.

Courage is a birthright.

Fearlessness of death insures the strongest love of life.

No one can know what it is to appreciate life at its best until he has ceased to have any suspicion of dread of death.

No one can realize the keenest enjoyment of life until he has grown to *feel—appreciate*—that this life is an important stage of an evolutionary process, in which the dawning of spiritual possibilities opens up the realm of divine existence to him, and introduces to his consciousness that *appreciation of God which gives birth to love, growth and happiness.*

When fearthought is entirely eradicated from the mind by the elimination of the basic fear—the fear of death—man begins to *feel* the responsibility of growing his best, of ripening in natural manner, and of dropping into the lap of Mother Earth only when he has instilled into himself the richest and sweetest juices of an appreciative and altruistic life.

Fear not Death if you would know and love life.

Mother-thought is the strongest of all thought.

Voluntary motherhood is the bravest of all acts common in life.

Whoever teaches a child to be fearless, builds greater than she can ever know, for fearlessness in one inspires courage in many; and as courage inspires strength and causes action, there is no end to what may grow out of the fearless influence of the frailest and physically weakest of women, and any young mother, in the quiet and seclusion of a modest home, can set in motion vibrations of strength and fearlessness that may result in the building of a great city or the invention of some world-emancipating tool of progress.

All great accomplishments can be traced back to mother-influence. Mother-muscle may be wanting, but mother-thought rules the world.

Mother-thought is always brave-thought in *one* emergency, and therefore *can be strong in all* emergencies.

Mother-thought rules the world.

Mother-thought blesses life.

All water is pure water.

It is impurities within water that muddy it.

All men are innately good.

It is the presence of false impressions, the result of false suggestions, that makes men selfish and bad.

There is no impurity in water that cannot be removed by some means within the reach of chemistry, and there is likewise no bad suggestion impressed on a sane human mind that cannot be counteracted by some right and good suggestion.

In your judgment of men, judge the sum of their opportunities and the quality of their environing atmosphere, and not the individuals themselves. It will aid you to a more just appreciation of the possible goodness of your neighbors, and greatly help to conserve your own happiness, through the diffusion of the warm blood of charitable impulse.

Mould conditions aright, and men will grow good to fit them.

The perfect man is the harmonious man.

The perfection of anything is dependent upon the perfection of all its parts.

Good society is made up of good individuals; individuals are measured by their qualities of mind and character; and mind and character are pure and good according as their constituent elements are pure and good.

Fearthought is a weak element of mind and its influence on character is blighting.

In chemistry and in mechanics we analyse and test with greatest care the material we use, to learn its value as related to our purpose. If it have any element of weakness we discard it.

Measure, and weigh well, thought about the future; if it partake of fearthought, expel it from the mind, for it is evil; if it be filled with strength, and hope, and confidence, nurse it tenderly, for it is good.

Harmony is strength.

***

Forethought is strong thought.

Fearthought is weak thought.

Nervousness is frequently discreditable, and, therefore, not-respectable.

Nervousness is the "scapegoat" for much cowardice, ignorance and perversion, sometimes of prenatal, but generally of post-natal, origin. It is not as respectable as scrofula, for the reason that scrofula may have been inherited or contracted by the accident or evil doing of another, and can be corrected only by process of regeneration; while nervousness is an expression or reflection of fearthought which can be corrected by one's own right-thinking.

Whoever is not nervous when he is asleep *need not be* nervous when he is awake.

Eminent physicians have recently authorized the above assertions relative to nervousness. If it is evil and unnecessary, it is, therefore, not-respectable.

When nervous, seek within the habit-of-thought for a cause.

Attraction rules the universe.

The rivalry between attraction and counter-attraction is friendly.

Evolution is the result of being attracted to increase and to growth, and not the result of being *pushed* to growth.

All plant life inclines towards the light and the sun.

Plant life that is strong enough to withstand the storms, turns its back in protest to the wind.

Pessimists snarlingly assert that attraction is the *pushing of desire* for change, but pessimists are diseased themselves, and therefore call things by wrong names, and give the wrong construction to everything.

Appreciation and resultant Love are caused by attraction, and not by fear.

Whatever is attracted forward or upward, will remain in advance or above.

Forethought is eagerly receptive and seeks progress through attraction.

Fearthought *pushes* to action by its own cowardice, and accomplishes nothing useful.

ALTRUISM IS A POWERFUL MAGNET; GOOD MEN ARE "AS TRUE AS STEEL."

Consideration is practical altruism.

Consideration for others is evidenced by desiring to do for them what is most desired by them, or, what is best for them. It *assumes* no superiority.

Consideration is "catching," and the easiest way to accomplish one's own desires, in connection with others, is to suggest consideration by consideration.

No one ever "lost a trick, or missed a meal," by being considerate; and simple, unaffected consideration has often been the means of adding great possessions to its own richness.

"After you," will unravel a crowd quicker than any pushing to be first.

Fearthought, and the selfishness growing out of it, are the origin of all lack of consideration for others; and contact with others, and the every-day amenities of life furnish constant opportunity for attacking one of the strongest expressions of the disease of fearthought by practice of altruistic consideration.

THE FIRST REQUISITE OF GENTILITY IS CONSIDERATION.

Happy Day!

"Good morrow," "good day," "good morning," and "good evening," were originally intended to have the same significance as our opening salutation, but now they have generally become stale and mean no more than "how are y——" "how d'y" and other perfunctory greetings that are ridiculous when rendered with an inflection that resembles a grunt.

Elsewhere it is related how "happy day" is used in some families to greet the morning.

What humanity is suffering from is a restriction of affections, and an effusion of fears.

People are afraid of being frank and therefore cultivate the sulks, suffer and become ill from the repression.

If you cannot greet the morning and likewise every living thing and every inanimate thing that there is with "Happy Day," you had better take medicine for the trouble, for you are really ill.

HAPPY DAY!

Forethought is Optimism.

All good men are optimists.

The contrastive definitions of "optimism," and "pessimism" and "content," as given by Rev. Dr. Newel Dwight Hillis in an address on optimism, which the author had the pleasure of hearing, are in themselves an epitome of good suggestion relative to the profitable attitude toward the past, the present and the future.

Said Dr. Hillis, "The pessimist cries, 'all is ill, and nothing can be well'; the idle dreamer assumes that 'all is well,' but the optimist declares that 'all has not been ill, and all has not been well—all is not ill, and all is not well—but all *can be* and therefore *shall be* well.'"

Appreciation of ever-present blessings—the sun, the birds, the perfume of the flowers, the mist, the constant changes in the aspect of nature, the love of friends, the hurdles that are met and cleared at a bound, and even the obstructions that Providence places in the *wrong road*, make them all seem to chant in chorus,—"No matter what has been; no matter what is; all *can be* and *shall be* well."

Optimism is life.

Fearthought inspires Pessimism.

Pessimism is a false prophet.

It would certainly seem to be in the interest of freedom if the utterances of evil foreboding and pessimistic prophesy were frowned upon, if pessimists were avoided as lepers are avoided, and if their effect on growth and development were to measure the merit or demerit of thoughts or teachings, as well as of actions.

Society's duty toward the individual is wisely to prevent him from doing harm, either to himself or to others. All experience teaches that pessimism is generally lying prophesy. To prohibit false prophesy, that can only injure both the maker and the hearer of it, would seem, then, to be not only the right, but the duty, of society. To prohibit bad suggestion as well as bad action, when action is known to be but materialized or realized suggestion, would seem to be a duty of society.

Pessimism is poison.

"Perfect Love Casteth out Fear."

But:

Perfect Love cannot exist until Fear is *first cast out.*

Forethought is essential to cultivation and happiness.

But:

Fearthought in forethought prevents cultivation and kills happiness.

Fear is Habit-of-Fearthought only, and is self-imposed, or imported.

It is, therefore:

UNNECESSARY.

Fearthought, being unnecessary, is a weak, or a cowardly, self-infliction.

It is, therefore:

NOT-RESPECTABLE.

Fearthought, the arch-enemy of mankind, can be eliminated from the Habit-of-Thought—can be entirely eradicated.

But:

NOT BY REPRESSION.

Man, equipped with *divine selection*, is the only cultivator in Nature. Nature does all growing herself, and assigns all cultivating to Man.

But:

He cultivates only through removing deterrents to growth.

Man's value, as assistant in evolution, consists in his ability to create harmonic conditions favorable to growth through the exercise of *divine selection*.

But:

He secures perfect harmony only by first harmonizing himself.

Happiness is "the aim and the end of existence."

But:

Happiness can rest only in Harmony, Appreciation, Love and Altruism.

Happiness is "The Greatest Thing in the World."

But:—If sought aright,

It is easier than not!

Suggestions in Menticulture.

Stop importing; or eradication versus repression

THE ATTITUDE of Man towards his weaknesses is commonly that of repression. He assumes that fearthought, and fear, and anger, and worry, and all of the evil passions are inherent things that may be repressed but not eradicated; modified but not eliminated; kept under partial control but not gotten rid of; and cut down below the surface, so as not to be exposed to the world, but not rooted out entirely.

By some persons it is even thought to be an accomplishment of great merit to acknowledge strong roots of carnal weakness and to then succeed in hiding any outward expression of them. In others, equally well-meaning, the aggressive and consumptive passions are nursed and exhibited as evidences of unusual sensitiveness and virility appertaining to fineness, goodness and greatness. It is not long since it was the custom of clergymen in some denominations to assume unworthiness for themselves in order to glorify the redeeming power of the Saviour, notwithstanding all of Christ's teachings inculcated that true forgiveness consisted in the simple process of *ceasing to have*—ceasing to admit, or import. When, in former times, priesthood was degraded to a business—an occupation for a living, or for convenience or power—it was natural that the difficulty of the service rendered the laity by the priests should be exaggerated so as to command the highest respect, the greatest power and the largest compensation. Sin was made to seem powerful and ever-present in order that the service rendered in keeping it in check might seem important and everlasting. Under such circumstances, and especially when the one great unpardonable sin against the church was that of doubting the teachings of these teachers, how almost impossible must it have been for the laity to rise superior to evil, when those whose profession it was to combat it, found it so potent an enemy, and who, thereby, filled the atmosphere of thought with dense clouds of evil suggestion.

It is fortunate for the present generation that such shadows of suggestion do not hopelessly oppress it. There are many churches now where appreciation, and love, and purity, and the delights of unselfishness are offered as the attractions towards religion, and where the teachers in them stand for examples of pure thinking, pure living, and spontaneous altruism, practiced as a result of natural impulses that are both agreeable and profitable, and not to save from hell or to fit for a remote heaven. But the shadow of the old method, that so long hid the Christ-method of true thinking and living, still has an influence in giving strength to evil to afflict the weaker sons of our civilization. This shadow, however, cannot long remain. The light of the present awakening is too strong—too electric and too penetrating—to permit it to remain.

It is even looked upon now as a curiosity—a relic of antiquity— to hear the old fears given expression from the pulpit, but root eradication of them is not yet insisted upon as the first and most important teaching, as it should be. It is a common thing now, also, to hear altruistic teaching and optimistic preaching from the pulpits of all denominations, and to hear from the teachers and preachers the assurance that "it is easier than not and more profitable in every way to be unselfish and not to tolerate evil," the new good suggestion of which, is the inspiring assertion that, "*it is easier than not.*"

It would be a rare thing now to find a religious teacher of intelligence who would not agree with the assertion that, when a person is angry, he cannot be, at the moment, a Christian, for being angry is as unchristian as profanity. The same condemnation applies to worry, which is especially commanded against, and which, in the light of the observed promises of God as expressed by the preponderance of the prevalence of good, is not less than blasphemous in its exhibition of lack of confidence in, and appreciation of, the Giver of All Good.

A most helpful thought in connection with the easy subjugation of the *animalesque* expressions of fearthought is, that they are not inherent things, and that they are imported whenever suffered. The tendency to import is inherent, and the *tendency* to entertain evil is the shadow of past error in the race which is called race-habit-of-thought, and it is that which has to be replaced by right-habit-of-thought before one is entirely free, but tendency is easily overcome when its parents are discredited and made not-respectable thereby.

The spiritual awakening of the present era that is reclaiming Christianity from the supernatural, or unnatural, and applying it to everyday affairs, may be called practical or business Christianity. A business man who has an occupation wherein it is possible for him to be altruistic, after reading the theory that is the contention of *Menticulture*, wrote a commentary in which he said: "On these precepts not only 'hang all of the law and the prophets,' but, also, common business sense and *all of the profits*."

As an illustration of the difference between eradication (or filtration) and repression (or gradual dilution or reform) I will cite a common example: Suppose a vessel to be filled with muddy water which we wish to make clear, so that it will perfectly reflect the ether above, which we call the sky; the easy and effective method is first to pass the water through a filter and thereafter to protect it from contamination. On the contrary, the difficult, expensive, endless and, therefore ineffective method is to pour unlimited clear water into the vessel, in order to gradually replace the muddy water with the excess of pure water.

While it is true that "perfect love casteth out fear," it also is true that there can be no perfect love until there is first perfect freedom from fear, so that the right way to approach the problem of creating the harmonious condition in the human mind wherein growth ripens in happiness, is to take the mind when it is returned to us at the moment of awaking from sleep, when it has been purified by contact with Spiritual Cerebration, and protect it from that time forth through each day, by refusing *to import* suspicion, anger or worry into it, a process that is *easier than not*, and pleasanter and more profitable than any.

Each day, the tendency to import, which is the only part of the process of eradication that is in any way real, will become less strong, and, with even the weakest attempts to discourage it; but if you are sufficiently in earnest to say, "Begone, you tempter," and thereby slam the door in his face, you will accomplish freedom at once.

The self-infliction of fearthought is a shoveling-in process—all that you have to do to become free from it is to stop shoveling. It is easier to stop importing fearthought, and anger, and worry, and suspicion, than it is to import them; therefore,

Stop importing!

The impotence of Pain.

DURING THE JAPANESE-CHINESE WAR, two Japanese students were arrested in Shanghai on the charge of espionage, and were taken to Ningpo and tortured to death.

The method of torture was the most cruel known, and included a slow crushing of the most sensitive parts of their anatomy.

The young patriots displayed such heroism under the torture that the incident gave rise to considerable discussion as to the relative sensitiveness of the Mongolian and the Caucasian races to pain. The consensus of the opinion that I saw expressed, which was, by the way, Caucasian opinion only, was that the Oriental was less sensitive, and therefore was not entitled to as much credit for withstanding pain as the self-adjudged, more-sensitive Westerner.

The truth of the matter is, that there is a limit to actual pain within the power of any one to endure, if the element of fearthought-of-more-pain is eliminated, so that the absorbing heroism of the patriot—almost courting torture for the honor of his cause—puts the element of fearthought out of the case, and leaves only the actual sensation to be suffered. Pain is undoubtedly intended as a warning of disordered conditions, and not as a punishment, and, having performed its mission, is relieved by a kind paralysis before the shock is too severe for human endurance.

This is the beneficent provision of the natural law, but when it comes to the exercise of unnatural fearthought, there is no limit to the torture a victim may impose upon himself, and, on a basis of a very little real pain, build up most terrible suffering.

The author has tested the truth of this assertion personally.

Being condemned to submit to a dental operation of unusual severity, the opportunity to experiment was gladly availed of, even at the expense of comfort.

One special aggravation of the operation was the prying open of the mouth, in order to build up from the root one of the teeth located farthest back in the mouth. The mouth was not large enough to suit the facile convenience of the dentist, and hence he made use of all the skill and power he possessed to enlarge the cavity, and having stretched it to the utmost, firm wedges held it open, without possibility of protest, for three hours on a stretch; and on these instruments and conditions of torture I had ample opportunity to experiment; so sufficient—for all practical purposes—that I do not feel it necessary to repeat the experiment, even in the interest of scientific investigation.

The experiment proved, however, my contention, that even the greatest possible pain is of itself not very severe, and that it requires but a slight diversion to make one forget it, for the time being, entirely. I was able, at any moment of the combined irritation, to concentrate my mind upon some subject or object, and to lose the sense of pain out of my consciousness altogether—and at will.

Major General O. O. Howard, U. S. A. (retired) has recently corroborated, to the author, out of his own experience, the possibility of forgetting pain through slight diversion. He lost an arm during the Civil War, and in the process of recovery some of the nerve-ends were not properly cicatrized, so that ever since the wound healed the General has not been free from the sensation of pain, whenever his mind has reverted to it, and yet he is able at any time to forget it by change of thought.

In like manner, fear-of-trouble is the major part of all the so-called trouble that is experienced. As intimated in the "definitions," under the caption of "Trouble," there are few real conditions that are very uncomfortable, if apprehension of still more uncomfortable conditions is not imported to exaggerate the existing discomfort. Fear of freezing to death or of drowning may be made very terrible, for instance, whereas the end in freezing and in drowning is known to be so comfortable, and even blissful, that those who are on the point of passing out of life by those means dislike to be called back to life again.

The heroism of mothers in the event of child-birth is too well known to call for reference, but there is the greatest difference in the ease or in the discomfort of the condition attending the process, which is largely influenced by the feeling of welcome or the attitude of aversion with which the new-comer is greeted by the mother.

The point-of-view has much to do with the sting of pain. Whoever has suffered that severest of all spankings, the water spanking incident to a clumsy dive, or a wrongly-calculated somer-sault into the water from a wharf, or from a natatorium springboard, will remember that the pain of it is not half so hard to bear as the form of parental correction called by the same name, that in itself is not nearly so severe.

Sensitiveness to pain is largely due to the fear of pain, and a reversal of the accustomed attitude towards fear will have an immediate effect upon the severity of pain by mitigating much of its sting. Christian scientists, mental scientists, spiritual scientists, faith curists, and all others who practice mental therapeutics in physical diseases, escape much suffering in this way, and the happy result of this attitude towards pain serves to strengthen their faith.

Whatever the cause of the relief, it is good, for it teaches, in a most practical way, the potency of thought in overcoming, or, dismissing, real pain as well as all imaginary evil, and also the possibility of eliminating fearthought from the mental equipment, by showing how impotent to harm are the realities that inspire it, when it is prevented from exaggerating them.

Unhappy unless miserable.

THERE ARE SOME PERSONS, in fact, a great many persons, who are not happy unless they have real or fancied cause for complaint. Martyrdom is the recreation of such people and they are liable to be more greedy for recreation than those whose recreation is of a joyous sort.

It is certainly a misplaced kindness to impose unwelcome attentions on any one. In the category of nuisances unwelcome attentions are perhaps the most disagreeable, and to cram joy down the maw of one who has no taste for it, is as rude, and even vulgar, as insisting that he shall eat something that is nauseating to him.

It is true that persons who gloat over misery; who love to mope about in grave-yards; and are forever telling grewsome tales for the supposed delectation of their victims, are not as agreeable to others as they seem to be to themselves, and their presence at festivals and other ostensibly joyous occasions may be looked on as discordant, and, as such, out of place.

In these times of license, which are sometime mistaken for times of unusual liberty, it is not for anyone to define what is altogether bad, nor to confine good, nor good taste, within too narrow limits; neither is it generous to prescribe anything that shall be universally eaten or worn; and, above all liberties, the liberty to wear a smile or a frown should prevail; but it is within the province of organized society to put its stamp of approval or disapproval on the time and place for appropriate use of them. Certain costumes are suitable in certain places and not suitable in others. For example, the bathing suit and the night-robe have uses that are appropriate for their special purposes, but they would not be tolerated on the street by the police, and it would be no greater curtailment of liberty to order that frowns shall be worn only in dark places and not be permitted to cloud the sunlight, than that undue levity should be tabooed on occasions considered to be serious. If such prescription were to be imposed, it would be necessary, of course, to furnish dark places at appropriate, or, rather, convenient intervals, for the use of the miserably inclined, in the same way that spittoons are provided for the use of those who must expectorate sputum.

Liberty is so precious a thing that it must be protected as the holiest of our possessions, and even if it lap over into the debatable ground sometimes called license, it should yet be protected, and therefore the permission to wear frowns in appropriate places and to enjoy being miserable in the privacy of one's own chamber should be respected; on the street, or anywhere in public, however, they should not be tolerated, for they are harmful generally, and particularly injurious to children.

As individuals, those of us who accept God's promises as truths, who prefer to live in the sunlight rather than in a cave, who glorify Appreciation as the first and best suggestion in the language, who believe that growth is the object of life, that its fallow field is harmony, and that its fruit is happiness, and also those of us who, by comparison of conditions have learned to believe that our pessimistic friends can be happier than they are, and can become better companions and citizens by a change of attitude towards life, although we may not pass laws of restriction against the frown-habit or against the misery-habit, can use the gentle method of counter-suggestion to good effect, and even go so far as to laugh at and otherwise ridicule the misery-habit, if by thus doing we may possibly correct that which logic has failed to cure.

From long observation it has become evident that the misery-habit feeds on sympathy. Children, who are the best examples of honest expression that we have, whereby to see ourselves in an unartificial light, will not continue a mad or a surly crying spell if they are sure it is not producing a sympathetic effect. If they think they are not heard they will at once cease crying. In the same way, grown persons who practice the misery-habit in public take a rest when they are unobserved. They try to hide it, but they are frequently caught in the act of unbuttoning their pouts, and thereby allowing their faces a rest, as soon as they have thought themselves out of sight. We must believe, if this observation be correct, that the object of pessimism, or, the misery-habit, is generally to secure, by dishonest means, selfish attentions that are not earned, and for which no value is given. There are cases no doubt where the misery-habit has been acquired by contact with respected ones who have been the cause of perverse suggestions too strong to be resisted, and for such there can only be pity, and in the cure of whom gentle and loving suggestion should be used, but to the perverse and the chronic practicers of the misery-habit, no toleration is good, for it is on that, and unmerited sympathy, that they live and thrive. On such, all of the misery possible to be scraped up from the discords of life should be dumped, and they should be condemned to herd together, and if it were possible, they should be isolated, as lepers are isolated, from healthy society.

Sometimes the victim of the misery-habit practices the habit only within the family. This is especially severe on the family, and is much more difficult to treat. The family is at once the seat of the greatest liberty, and the home and breeding-ground of the greatest tyranny. The family is supposed to be under the holy protection of the divine principle of love, but if that principle is not a possession of the family, there is no protection whatever from most inhuman practices, but instead a license to the cultivation of most discordant passions. It is in the family that mollygrubs are grown and tolerated. It is in the family that one cannot get rid of them by running away, for the family, like the poor, you have with you always. And who would have it otherwise? The whole tendency of civilization is to appreciate the family more and more, and to cultivate respect for the family model as the basis of good government. But it is the very security of the natural, and therefore indissoluble, bonds that gives the selfishly inclined opportunity to practice the misery-habit without fear of being thrown out, left behind, cremated or otherwise gotten rid of, as dead and disagreeable matter is usually treated, in civilized communities.

The symptoms of the misery-habit, or martyr-habit, are easy to detect, for while they may be cultivated and laboriously practiced in private, they are intended to be seen, and are displayed at times when they are calculated to be most conspicuous. The victim of the martyr-habit is usually an industrious person. He, or possibly she, will perform any amount of necessary, and even unnecessary, manual labor, in order to exhibit martyr-like fatigue; is always hanging behind in order to be slighted; condemns attentions honestly intended as perfunctory politeness; interprets praise as being patronage; finds any part of a chicken served him at the family table the worst piece, and at the same time assures the carver that he has been unduly partial or over-generous—but, with a tone of voice or an expression of countenance that belies the utterance. A common phrase of the afflicted martyrite is, "Don't mind me," and hysterics is the favorite amusement, while pain and trouble are the chief stock in trade. And is there a remedy? Yes.

If Christianity were to be measured by the optimism of the Master, if the gauge of optimism prescribed by the Master were to be used to measure professing Christians for the name; if cause and effect were to be placed in their true relation to each other, and the ills we cultivate were to be classed as self-imposed causes and not effects; and if the unnecessary and unprofitable were to be ranked as not-respectable; the misery-habit or martyr-habit would cease to be fashionable, mollygrubs would disappear, and the principal breeding-ground of pessimism—the family—would be purified, as becoming to its holy office.

Thou shalt not strike a woman.

IF A QUEER SORT of human being, dressed in a costume we had never seen before, and hailing from some island we had never heard of, were to land on our shores and ask our protection and the privilege of teaching the religion of his people; if he were to learn our language sufficiently to convey his ideas to us; if he were to have printed the formulas of his religion, and, among them, his deity's commandments to men; if the first of these commandments were to read, "Thou shalt not strike a woman," what would we say to such a commandment? and what would we think of a people who found it necessary to have such a formula?

Our question would naturally be, "Do the people of your country *ever* strike women?"

In our particular state of chivalric civilization, striking women is one of the things so entirely out of the question that we do not consider it even a possibility, except in cases of insanity or of drunkenness, where the brute of the moment is not responsible for his action.

The very fact of its being an impossible, and therefore unmentionable, crime is the strongest suggestion against it.

If "Thou shalt not strike a woman" were listed in the category of commandments, and were constantly repeated as something hard to resist, and hence commanded against, I believe the crime would become common in circles where it is not thought of as possible now.

The best thing to do with a condemned thing is to cover it up, seal it up, and relegate it to the custody of the awful, unwritten law of unanimous disapproval.

It is said that when the Jesuit fathers went to Japan at the end of the sixteenth century they were warmly welcomed, and not only were permitted but invited to teach their religion.

One of the first things they did was to have the ten commandments of the old Mosaic law printed in Japanese, in the form of what we call a tract, and distributed among the people.

Reading was then, as now, a common accomplishment with the Japanese, and they were interested in the tract. They did not quite understand its purport, however, and one of their number was delegated to ask for an explanation.

Japan is the land, above all others, where poetry and flowers and idealism and art and other refinements are cherished and appreciated. Poetry, in Japan, is sometimes so idealistic that it is somewhat vague to any but the poet. It is the custom, therefore, to consider that anything not quite comprehensible must be poetry; and not understanding the tract of the fathers, the Japanese naturally thought it to be a specimen of Portuguese poetry.

Approaching one of the fathers, the spokesman of the people bowed with accustomed politeness and said: "I trust you will pardon the wretched ignorance and dullness of my humble self, but the great interest of my companions, as well of myself, in your poem, impels us to ask you to interpret to us the great depth of its beauteous crystalline sweetness, in order that we may enjoy it as it is worthy of being enjoyed."

The father was shocked to hear his sacred commandments classed as worldly poetry, and, drawing himself up to the full impressiveness of holy indignation, replied, "That is not poetry; that is what our God commands that we *must not* do."

"Sayo de go zarimasu, gomen na sai," answered the spokesman in the polite idiom of his country; "but—*do the people of your country ever do these things?*"

Whether the Japanese are, or were three hundred years ago, as exempt from evil as the enquiry about the ten commandments would imply, matters not. The rebuke was well merited and taught a great, good lesson. We are the sum of our impressions, and the suggestions we receive from experience are the source of our impressions. Some suggestions are so respected that they make deep impressions, notably the suggestions given us by our parents at our most impressionable age; but all suggestions have some weight, and to such purpose that a thing we know to be untrue becomes a reality to us by constant repetition, as attested by the common expression, "He has told that story so many times that he has come to believe it himself."

There is scarcely any difference of opinion about the justice of the ten commandments; but the constant repetition of *"you must not"* is like shaking a red rag before a wild bull, to many self-assertive children; whereas, if the things to be commanded against were understood to be *impossible*, and therefore *unmentionable*, the commandments would come to fit crimes that had become as much out of date to us now as is the crime of striking women.

We have constant evidence of the fact that beliefs, or, rather, habits-of-belief, follow persistent assertion, and that character is largely molded by existing formulas as well as other influences of our environment.

Without desire to criticise the formulas of any creeds, except in the way of counter-suggestion, I would ask, "What would be the probable effect of teaching the constant repetition of the eleventh commandment in place of the older ten?—'A new commandment I give unto you, that you love one another.'" It is impossible to love and to hate at the same time. It is impossible to obey the eleventh commandment and disobey any of the ten at the same time. Is it not better practice of suggestion, in order to form habit-of-thought, to repeat the eleventh commandment eleven times, than to repeat each of the ten once and the eleventh only once?

It is true that the easy way to attain good is to *cease to have evil*, but, it is a poor way to cease to have evil to nurse it in the memory as a thing *difficult not to have.*

If there is to be repetition of anything, it is better that it should be of such suggestions as "Appreciation" and "Love."

The mind is as amenable to the force of habit as are any of the physical members of the body. The soul is much more amenable to suggestion than either, for it is much more impressionable. If you were teaching a child to play the piano, would you have him run all the scales, or, rather, combinations of notes that do not form scales, that are to be avoided in music, in order to teach him the habit of *not* playing them? Would it be good teaching to have him habituate his fingers to the sequence of false scales as well as to the sequence of true scales? May not the constant repetition of the commandments that refer to lewd practices suggest thoughts about lewdness that never would come to young minds by other means, and therefore taint pure thought, in brutal fashion, by vile suggestion?

The point-of-view.

SUPPOSE two men of equal physical strength were to start in a thousand-mile bicycle race. Suppose one of the men were to greet the passing of each mile-post in this wise: "Only nine hundred and ninety-nine miles more; only nine hundred and ninety miles more," or whatever the distance covered might be at the time. Suppose the other were to greet the same mile-posts otherwise, as "only one mile;" or, "hang it, only ten miles." Which racer would win?

In effect, one of the men would be going down hill and the other would be going up hill, and just that difference of approach would win the race for the person who was rolling down from one thousand miles to one mile, from the person who was struggling along the upward course from one mile to a thousand miles.

Suppose two men were to each feel a pain in the joint of his big toe. Suppose one of the attacked ones were to greet the pain as follows: "Well! I suppose that means the gout, and I am to be afflicted for the balance of my life with that horrible disease. What have I done to deserve such a fate? I suppose some of my ancestors are responsible for this, but I will have to suffer for it all the same." Suppose the other victim were to greet the same symptom in himself differently, as follows: "Hello, old fellow, what does all this mean?— too much rich food, too much rich wine, too much of everything that is good to the taste and bad for the stomach. Well, I might have expected it. Am ever so much obliged to you, Mr. Pain, for having warned me so promptly; I'll take the hint and correct the error before the trouble gets seated. Keep me well posted, Mr. Pain. If the disorder does not disappear, please keep on prodding me so that I will know if I am doing the right thing or the wrong thing towards it." Which of these men would recover more quickly, and which of them would suffer more discomfort?

There are always different points-of-view and different attitudes towards every problem of life. The different points-of-view are always in competition, and, other conditions being equal, winning or losing is a question of attitude. The attitude that is directed by appreciation, gratitude, hope, trust, or any of the attributes of Forethought, will always win, as against the attitude that is handicapped by any shade of Fearthought.

Life may be filled with disappointments or with successes merely by the choice of point-of-view, the pessimistic point-of-view leading from disappointment to disappointment, and the optimistic point of view leading to a succession of successes. As a man thinks, so does he act, and so does the world help him to act.

Evolution never places obstacles in the *right* road. A seeming obstacle may be but a hurdle, the clearing of which may win a prize in the life race. Some one has said that the supreme obstacle in life is surmounted by aid of the progressively difficult smaller obstacles that are overcome with increasing ease, and which, if their beneficent uses are known, become only hurdles instead of obstructions.

"Set 'em up again; they are all down but nine," said, in the spirit of hopeful determination, has won games for many contestants.

It is the point-of-view that determines whether an obstacle is a hurdle or an obstruction, or whether the obstruction, if it be such, is in the *wrong* road or not. If a traveler on life's road starts with an optimistic point-of-view he will enjoy obstacles as hurdles, or he will greet obstructions with pleasure, as being Providentially placed in the *wrong* road. In any case he will be happy about it, and his happiness will be the best possible stimulant in aiding him to clear hurdles or to seek new paths to pleasant places.

The optimistic and pessimistic points-of-view are the means by which the concordant and discordant notes in life are sounded. The merit or demerit of things lies less within the things themselves, as far as the observer is concerned, than in his ability to accept them complacently, if inevitable, and to mould or to shape them to profitable and agreeable uses, rather than to suffer them as unprofitable and disagreeable. For example, it is profitable to look upon all persons and upon all experiences as teachers, but to reserve the superiority of choosing to be guided by them or warned by them according as the quality of the teaching is good or bad.

There are proverbs in all languages that teach the preference of the optimistic point-of-view, but they will avail little as long as fearthought is tolerated as a necessary and respectable thing. Experience endorses the proverbs and discredits the necessity and respectability of fearthought.

The Japanese have a proverb, born of the optimistic point-of-view, that is very useful to them, inasmuch as the light wood-construction of their houses invites frequent fires and sweeping losses in consequence. After a fire it is fashionable in Japan for sufferers to greet each other in sympathy with the truism, always accompanied by a smile, "Not much trouble to move," and then they all pitch in to assist as much as possible to rehabilitate each other through kind attentions that really make the fires but hot-bed nurseries of altruistic sympathy, in which there is more joy than in the greatest accumulation of possessions.

After the war—the recent sectional dispute, whose theater of destruction was in the Southern States of America—many of the families of the ante-bellum slave aristocracy were mainly reduced in possessions, and deprived of some of the means of ostentation, and in rare instances, of the necessary means of comfort; but they had been defeated in their Cause, and many of them settled into a state of depression that was more cruel to them than all the reverses of the war. Nature continued to be as kind, the seasons smiled on the crops with unvarying regularity, and the physical scars of war were soon healed and overgrown, but the disappointed ones heeded not the return of material prosperity. They focused their point-of-view upon the past, and refused to see the smiles and the warmth of the present and the promise of the future.

Property aristocracy always creates a false pride, in which the point-of-view is distorted.

It will undoubtedly be the same with the name-proud Greeks as it was with the property-proud Southrons, and bespeaks little for the respectability of a pride that afflicts its victims more seriously than the destruction of property.

It is a meritorious pride that rises superior to defeat, and after saying "Thy Will Be Done" adds, "Teach Thou Me Appreciation," and begins the pursuit of peace anew with the point of view directed by optimism and not by pessimism.

I have seen whole families, suffering from self-imposed humiliation and depression, leap into new life, new growth, and new happiness at a change of the point-of-view. The Southerners are, above all other Americans, chivalrous and loyally American in their natures. They are also generally religious, and cling to the teachings of their parents. In focusing their point-of-view upon the past, and, nursing the sting of defeat, they have thought that they were conserving filial regard, chivalry and religion, and they have held to the distorted point-of-view with loyal purpose. A change of the point-of-view, rising superior to disappointment, more nearly satisfied filial pride, while Christian optimism and gratitude more nearly became the profession of religion than the fault-finding dictated by the antiquated point-of-view. Finding fault with the happenings of the past is as much blasphemy as any other disapproval of the Almighty, and yet blasphemy is regarded as the wickedest of sins in religious estimation; and, at the same time, loading up with a burden of depression and self-humiliation is the most unprofitable form of self-abuse known to economics.

It is better to have an intelligent and optimistic command of the point-of-view and hold title to nothing, than to have possessions valued at millions, and not count this as the richest possession of them all. If anything seem to be wrong with you, first examine the point-of-view. If you do this conscientiously, you will probably find the fault therein and seek a remedy by *changing the point-of-view.*

Don't be a sewer.

A SEWER IS a channel for the conveyance of disagreeable matter.

Any person who receives and carries mean report or suspicion of his neighbor is therefore a human sewer.

A good sewer is a good thing. It receives disagreeable matter and carries it along, hidden from sight and away from the other senses, to some remote place, and discharges it there.

A leaky sewer is an abomination.

Human sewers usually leak. They take delight in letting out the disagreeable matter they are carrying, at every street corner, in every parlor, and in the midst of the multitude, wherever they may chance to be. The characteristic of the human sewer is that it is a leaky sewer. By its leaks it is known.

Human sewers themselves generally create much of their sewage.

I once had a friend, an otherwise good fellow, who had acquired the habit of collecting and distributing social sewage. He was not amenable to logical suggestion against the habit. He held the idea that a spade should be called a spade, and that if disagreeable things existed, honesty required that they should be discussed. One day, when my friend was carrying an unusually heavy load of sewage, and was distributing it freely, this thought came into my mind, and I gave it utterance. "You remind me of a sewer," said I.

There might have been a serious impairment of our friendship as the result of my utterance, for my friend is full of so-called "spirit," had I not immediately followed my offensive remark by an apology, and a brotherly explanation somewhat in the vein as above.

The good effect of the comparison on my friend is my excuse for introducing it here. What logic and persuasion had not been able to accomplish, offensive comparison accomplished.

My friend is too self-respecting to allow himself to be in any way related to a leaky sewer, and has reformed beautifully. A short time since, in speaking of the incident, he acknowledged its effectiveness by saying, "Every time I think of anything mean I fancy I can smell it."

Call suspicion a liar.

IT IS an excellent rule to follow to call Suspicion a liar five times before basing judgment upon its testimony.

If you will take the trouble to investigate the average accuracy of your suspicions, you will note that they are wrong in so many cases that they are not a safe guide, and are generally unjust accusers.

While the person who harbors the suspicion is the worst sufferer in the end, when the accusations have been proved to be groundless, there is always a possibility of injustice, that, falling on servants or others holding inferior positions, is exceedingly cruel.

How often, in the household or in the hotel apartment, is a carelessly mislaid ring the cause of great unhappiness to both mistress and maid, because of the ready mischief of Fearthought and its attendant imp, Suspicion.

It is an axiom of the detective service, that untrained suspicion generally takes the wrong scent, and that it usually saves time to look in some other direction for the culprit, than in that pointed out by the accuser.

The elimination of the seeds of Fearthought from the mind, the possibility of which is the contention of my theory, will carry with it suspicion, and relieve one of endless chance of doing and suffering injustice, but if emancipation should, unfortunately, not have been accomplished, it is an excellent rule to follow, to meet Suspicion with suspicion, and call it "liar"! five times, before making accusation on its testimony.

I can't not do it.

A PERSON more frequently lies when he says "I can't" than when he says "I can." There are, to be sure, more things that one cannot do than there are that he can do, because the ability of the strongest and most skillful is comparatively limited; but the person who is in the habit of saying "I can't" usually says it about the wrong thing or at the wrong time.

Whenever a person says that he cannot do a thing that God has made it possible for him to do, and which he knows to be possible, he is not only a liar, but also a blasphemer.

If one is asked to climb a tree or lift a very heavy weight, there may be reason for saying "I can't," because of lack of ability, strength or practice. For the same reason, difficult "runs" on a piano, perilous feats of balancing or turning in gymnastics, and even a great many simple things that are easy to the accustomed, may be impossible to the unaccustomed without certain practice, and with reference to them it is reasonable to say, "I can't."

If, however, one is asked *not* to climb a tree, or *not* to lift a weight, or *not* to perform a "run" on a piano, there is no excuse for saying, "I cannot *not* do it," for it is as illogical as it is ungrammatical, and as false as any other lie.

Applied to mental accomplishment, it is even more illogical and false, because thought is more pliable than muscle.

Not being evil is simply *not being evil*, and whoever says, "I cannot *not* be bad," is a liar. When he is asleep he proves the lie.

There are habits-of-desire which seem attractive to perverted taste, that may need a strong counter-suggestion to correct, but there is no habit-of-desire but what can easily be corrected by the right counter-suggestion. For instance, drinking whisky habitually is recognized to be a bad habit of perverted desire, but one habitual drunkard I know of abjured whisky for life on account of having discovered a dead fly in his glass.

Sometimes it requires a mania to cure a mania. Dr. H. Holbrook Curtis, the eminent throat-specialist of New York, who has in his care, during grand opera season, millions of dollars' worth of voices, and who makes special study of the mental condition of his patients, once said to me, "The only cure that I know of for dipsomania is religio-mania." This same assertion is frequently made in quite a different way, but to the same effect. Dr. Curtis did not mean by religio-mania religious *appreciation*; neither did he mean by dipsomania, temperate use of stimulants. He referred to the intemperate emotion and the morbid taste. The practice of drinking unduly because of the social temptation of it may be cured by logical suggestion, but a mania may be amenable only to a mania. There is, however, no bad habit but that can be corrected by *some* means, and as there is some remedy for every separate phase of evil, it should be considered not respectable to say, "I cannot *not* do"; and, as measure of respectability is the highest social desideratum in the present age, the best weapon to be used against the toleration of evil in one's self or in others is a general protest against it on the score of its being unnecessary and not-respectable.

In my experiments I have used all sorts of means of suggestion with which to reach perverse habits of evil thought. As stated elsewhere, offensive comparisons and ridicule are more frequently effective than reason or logic, and, as such, are often necessary, in the same way that offensive medicines are sometimes effective in removing indigestible matter from the stomach,—for example, ipecac.

I had a friend who was in the habit of saying "I can't" to almost everything. The habit-of-opposition was so strong that it was the first to assert itself on every occasion. The attitude of opposition was strengthened by the perverse idea that brutal frankness is an expression of honesty, and hence reference to his honesty or dishonesty was a tender point of etiquette with my friend. To touch this tender spot, and administer the strong suggestion—medicine—necessary in the case, I hit upon this expedient:

Whenever my friend said "I can't" to a proposition which it did not fit, I immediately ejaculated "Liar!" At first there was some danger attending my experiment, but I took the precaution to be out of reach, and the fact that my intention was good assured me ultimate pardon.

At first my offensive criticism was frequently necessary, but it became less and less so, till at last the cure is so complete that the once favorite expression, "I can't," is as disagreeable to my friend, as must have been the dead fly in the glass of the drunkard previously mentioned, that was the means of curing him of a deeply rooted habit.

A million to one on the unexpected.

ONE EVENING, at a meeting of the "Ganglionics," in the city of New Orleans, I asked the president of the club, Dr. William Benjamin Smith, the question, "Why is it that the unexpected generally happens?" His reply, which induced the caption to this chapter, was, "Because the expected is only one thing, while the unexpected may be a million things."

This is really, as well as figuratively, true, and, being true, what idiots are we to waste our time and paralyze our energies, by thinking fearthought into the future, on a million-to-one chance of its hitting the mark.

There is one bull's-eye that we are sure to hit if we aim at it constantly and long enough. Death is the one universal bull's-eye that figures in every life. At the same time that we are sure of hitting it, we know by the experience of others that we do not realize death when it actually comes, for Nature kindly administers an anæsthetic just before death, and sometimes long before. Then why should we fear even death?

Persons who have been at the open door of the unexplored state called death say that a delightful feeling of rest comes over the emigrant, and that entry into the next state is like being in a beautiful dream.

If this be so, there is also nothing disagreeable in death—only in the fearthought about it—and hence the one only bull's-eye we have been sure of hitting—the cause of fear of death—does not exist, except in our hopes or our fears.

Many persons who are in the habit of apprehending cause for fearthought about the future, and who spend much of their time in worry, would not like to be put down in the category of false prophets, and yet their apprehension must be false in the ratio of chances of a million to one.

Thought about chance, as related to forethought, and from the point-of-view of the speculator or gambler, suggests the absurdity of wasting any good coin—calm and happiness—by "laying it on"—betting on—fear. The chances against having "coppered" the right fear are not only *not even*, but are ten to one against—an hundred to one against—or more—never less. Even if you should win by correctly guessing a fear, you would get back again none of the happiness that you had sacrificed—would not even get your "stake" back.

As a matter of actual experience, the following incident is a good example: A young man employed in a publishing house, where the proprietor was afflicted with the fuss-and-fret-habit, contracted the disease, and unconsciously became a victim to its toils. Robust good health began to give way to languor that induced dyspepsia and other contingent disorders, until suicide stared the young man in the face and haunted his dreams.

One day some one whispered a suspicion in the young employee's ear that was directed at worry and anger as the causes of his ill-health and unhappiness and the thought led his systematic habits-of-business to suggest "keeping tab" on at least one of the suspects, to see if it were the liar and thief, as charged. Each day, when worry made its predictions, record of them was carefully kept, and at the end of the month the reports were checked up by results. *Only three per cent. of the predictions were even remotely realized!*

The old proprietor of the business, through whom the contagious poison started, is dead, and the happy young menticulturist owns the business, which has become very successful by influence of the sunny optimism of its new owner, which attracts trade unconsciously to it.

Love cannot be qualified.

THE MERIT of loving is in the act, and should not—cannot—be qualified by the merit or demerit of the object under consideration.

There may be more effort required, perhaps, in loving something that seems to us unlovely, but no more virtue in so doing, as loving, like virtue, is its own reward.

God-love does not discriminate. It is, therefore, ungodly to discriminate. In the performance of the Man-Nature partnership-function of "divine selection" in the harmonizing of things that are antagonistic to each other and to Man—selecting for survival those things that are not deterrent to the harmonious growth and happiness of Man—if selection is to be made, it should be done in the spirit of calm justice, and not in the spirit of hate, for, as love blesses the lover, so does hate react upon the hater.

We cannot afford *not to love.*

There are animals and insects that seem to us to be undesirable and prejudicial to the harmony we are seeking to secure, that may serve most excellent purposes in relation to existing conditions. They are frequently a warning against unfavorable conditions, in the same way that pain is a warning against diseased conditions in the body. In the same way, crime is a warning against social or political conditions which invite or compel crime, and remedy should be sought in change of the conditions in preference to the punishment of the crime. I believe that a change of our point-of-view—our attitude towards causes and effects—would find punishment generally unnecessary, and, as such, brutal.

There is, then, a double reason why we should hate nothing. In the first place, it is probable that we are hating the wrong thing, and thereby are unjust, and we are certainly doing injury to ourselves by nursing the feeling of hatred.

Disapproval—calm disapproval—is a better judge in the exercise of "divine selection" than angry antagonism. Pity, as well as love, is a divine attribute, but hate is an attribute of the devil. Pity suggests change of conditions producing inharmonious results. Hate suggests punishment of the victim of the inharmony.

In its relation to personal comfort, the practice of not permitting hate, nor annoyance, nor irritation, nor repulsion to possess one's feelings, will bring greatest good results. Take the mosquito pest, for instance: One who begins to feel irritation at the sound made by the wings of the insect, is already creating within himself a condition favorable to inflammation from the effects of the bite. Many who suffer by mosquitos admit that the buzz is worse, to them, than the bite, which is proof of a purely mental and unnecessary affliction.

There was a time in my boyhood when mosquitos poisoned and annoyed me beyond endurance. Each bite represented a great itching welt, and the buzzing was full of terror in consequence, or, more likely, in the light of present knowledge, the buzzing inspired fearthought or dread, and the bite was very poisonous in consequence. At present, mosquito bites are not poisonous to me, and mosquito sounds are no longer disagreeable. I do not remember when the deliverance came. Possibly the cure came through intimate acquaintance. I have lived in localities where the mosquito thrives all the year round, and in such numbers that he tires his victims into a state of non-resistance, and in the calm of non-resistance, physical and mental irritations cease. This is sometimes called acclimatization, but it proves the contention, whichever way it is interpreted.

In the practice of my freedom from what was once a great affliction, I sometimes brave a swarm of mosquitos by sleeping in their presence without drawing the bar. If the mosquitos light on me freely, I find comfort in the evidence of my popularity, and in the fact that I am probably being of service to something, or somebody, by possibly diverting attentions that would not be appreciated in like manner by them. In the morning, when I look in the glass and note the little red spots that the bites have left, but of which I am not otherwise conscious, I consider them as a record of my hospitality, and am proud of them, as the German corps student is proud of the scars on his face, that are a record of equally foolish bravery or exposure, taken out of his university course at Heidelberg or elsewhere. My braving of the mosquitos would certainly be classed as foolish, except as a test of superiority, but the pin-point red spots soon disappear and do no permanent harm.

Mosquitos are said to breed in malarial conditions, and for the purpose of absorbing the malaria. Flies do not exist except in conditions of ferment, and are of greatest service in carrying it away. Roaches are splendid scavengers, and are a result, and not a cause, of unclean conditions. Our warfare should be waged against unclean and inharmonious conditions, and not against the purifiers and harmonizers of the conditions.

It is not a difficult matter to rid one's self of repulsions if the point-of-view is changed. I presume that the most generally detested creature that is not altogether deadly in its venom is the bedbug. The bedbug is more of a tradition than a fact, and many of those who shudder at mention of him have never seen one of his kind. I am sure that none of his enemies have much if, any, acquaintance with him, as to the color of his eyes, his habits of thrift, his amiability in his family and other qualities that serve to make a creature attractive and respectable within his sphere.

The truth about this much despised creature is that he is useful as a warning against unclean conditions, and his odor and his bite are his notes of warning. Instead of filling one's self with a feeling of repulsion or anger or any other emotion that affects the free circulation of the blood, and relaxes and disorders the tissues of the body, at sight or mention of a bedbug, the discovery should elicit the expression, "Thank you for the information." If it should happen in one's own house, no hidden crack nor corner should escape an overhauling to get rid of the cause of the bedbug's warning; or, if it should happen in a hotel, there should be a change of hotel.

Mention is made of mosquitos and roaches and bedbugs in this connection, not for the purpose of degrading the feeling of love by applying it to things that are disagreeable, no matter what their mission of usefulness, but to put stress upon the fact that one cannot afford to hate anything. It is especially useful, in seeking to change the point-of-view, to consider the greatest of causes of repulsion in order to more easily reach the lesser causes, for the lesser fade of themselves by the removal of the greater.

If you can learn not to hate a bedbug, to thank a roach for informing you of unclean conditions and to endure mosquitos, you are pretty sure to modify all prejudices by thus doing.

Last sometimes first.

IT IS my own habit to read the last chapter of a book first and if the summary of its contentions and deductions, which are sure to be found in the closing chapter, interest me, I go carefully through the book with the author to learn how he has reached his conclusions. I find, upon enquiry, that many others do the same. This is made necessary because of the vast number of books that are published and the impossibility of learning by other than the easiest means more than a small proportion of the ideas that are given out each year. There are published, yearly, in English, twenty to thirty thousand volumes of new matter, or new arrangements or new editions of old matter, so that to read carefully only a catalogue of them would be a considerable task for the ordinary reader.

This being the closing chapter of my book, and being especially possessed of my subject and desirous of being understood, I may be pardoned for offering a brief syllabus of my effort as a benediction.

I have endeavored to show that fearthought is the arch-enemy of civilized man. Through the fears of his progenitors, it is the cause of the weaknesses he inherits; and through his own permission, it is also the cause of his personally acquired ill health, ill success, discontent and unhappiness. Fearthought, however, can be eradicated from the habit-of-thought of even the most timid persons, who are cursed by the hereditary affliction of fear, or by their own weak habit-of-thought, by persistent counter-suggestion, as soon as they are convinced of the possibility of freedom, and have thereby, learned the profitable point-of-view regarding it. I have shown that forethought becomes strong-thought as soon as fearthought, or weak-thought, is separated from it; that the condition of harmony which is created by the eradication of fearthought, is the normal condition in civilized nature; that growth is immediate and strong within the harmonic atmosphere thus created; that happiness is the certain result; and that fearthought and its various expressions are the basic deterrents to growth and happiness in man. That God, in the process of Evolution, has developed Man to the point where he executes the Higher Law of Harmony through the exercise of Divine Selection in modifying the brute law of "the survival of the fittest" (or, strongest), and thereby proves the "superiority of mind over matter." That God has created a partnership between Growth and Man, which is properly distinguished as the Man-Nature partnership. That the functions of the partners are clearly defined by rigid limitations; Nature doing all the growing without harmonizing or cultivating anything; while Man performs all of the harmonizing or cultivating, but none of the growing. That Man's only method of harmonizing or cultivating is through learning and removing the deterrents to growth. That in watering plants, Man removes the deterrent, drouth. That in building hot-houses, Man removes the deterrent, cold. That in oiling machinery, Man removes the deterrent, friction. That in refusing to be the bondman of fearthought and anger and worry, Man escapes the only deterrents within himself, to harmony, health, growth and happiness. And, that in cultivating Appreciation all of the possibilities of Happiness are opened to him.

I have tried to show that one of the great deterrents to growth and the acquisition of happiness is nursed by focussing the point-of-view on worn-out traditions, instead of on the present accomplishments and acceleration of progress in which all of the elements of happiness rest. That while happiness is possible to all under present conditions, indications point to the possibility, within the assured possession of surplus wealth-of-means, that Altruism may soon "have an inning," during which conditions will be so rearranged that dire poverty and unhappiness will be impossible to any but the perverse. That normal, civilized human nature is *good* nature, and that if conditions are intelligently arranged most men will eagerly mold themselves into good men to fit the conditions. That the Material Age has become so rich that it can now afford leisure to give attention to the Higher Self, and in so doing will soon refuse to permit any one born under the prejudices and the protection of the Nation—the social family—to be ignorant nor idle nor poor; that the era of the three great A's—Appreciation, Attraction and Altruism—is upon us, and that it will inaugurate the Age of the Higher Self, wherein Man will realize that he is not simply the highest among animals, but is endowed with divine possibilities, and cannot longer be respectable with only animal characteristics. That the resetting of the gauge of respectability rendered necessary by the Awakening, and the new conditions that must grow out of it, will be above the toleration of anything that is unaltruistic, as surely as the gauge of the present is above the toleration of petty thieving and convicted perjury.

There is not only hope, but there *is assurance*, of harmonic conditions in the signs of the times and in the constantly increasing acceleration of progress.

A beginning and not an end.

IT IS ARGUED that the Stoics and other philosophers of ancient Greece attained the perfection of self-control, and successfully suppressed, and even eliminated, all of the passions and desires which so commonly dominate man, and attained thereby a state of happiness that is quite unknown in the present times of ostentation and ambition; but that the result was a state of lethargic indifference, that became more fatal to growth and progress in the end than any known condition of tumult and competition in the history of the race.

This is undoubtedly a just arraignment of the result of the Grecian philosophical teachings but, at the same time, the reason for so unhappy a result is not difficult to find.

The Greeks cultivated self-control and the harmonic conditions growing out of it as an end, and not as a preparatory means to growth. They prepared a weedless and wormless soil within the mind, but in it planted poppies, breathed of their poisonous perfume, and slept the sleep of indifference, which leads to the sleep called death.

Since the time of the Stoics, the world has been told by the God-Man Jesus of Nazareth, that living means growing, that true happiness is gained only through works in the service of something, that the necessary attribute of perfect manhood is spontaneous altruism,

and that there is no other road towards growth, refinement, spiritu-
ality and happiness than along the way made easy by consistent
altruism.

During the time that has passed since the power and glory of
Hellas began to wane, mankind has had experience with the forces of
nature and the efficacy of machinery to teach the great universal law
of compensation, which is also the law of happiness. This great law
prescribes that there shall be no balance without support or motion,
no poise without alertness, no life without growth, and no happiness
without service.

Learning a wise lesson from the law of compensation, man has
come to appreciate the value of a wormless and weedless soil, but he
has learned to plant in it trees that bear altruistic fruit, instead of the
poppy of sloth and indifference, which is now classed as a poisonous
weed; he has learned to clean and polish the journals of his engines
and has invented balance wheels to regulate, and ball bearings to
accelerate, their power; but not for the purpose of idleness.

The decadence of Greek manhood was not the result of culture,
but the result of the uses to which it was put, and hence we should
not condemn culture, nor cultivate friction, as an antidote for decadence, because Greek civilization did not defend itself against
assault and decay, but, rather, let us emulate the good they achieved,
and cultivate the power they attained, and use them as *a beginning
and not as an end.*

Appendices.

Appendix A.

THE INFLUENCE OF FEAR IN DISEASE

BY DR. WM. H. HOLCOMB.

OUR SANITARIANS ARE DOING a good work in exploring the physical causes of disease, and endeavoring to protect the individual and the public health. But there is a higher and larger sphere of causes which they have seldom penetrated, and of whose existence even many of them seem to be ignorant. I allude to the extraordinary influence of affection and thought, or of emotion and ideas, in the causation and prevention of disease.

The body is a mirror, in which all the states of the soul are reflected. We are familiar with the wonderful effects of the will, the passions, the emotions, of the imagination, sympathy, hope, fear, faith, and confident expectation upon the physical system. We are accustomed to regard the phenomena as illustrations of the fact that the soul can, under certain circumstances, act powerfully upon the body, with the tacit assumption, however, as a general rule, that the body executes all the functions by chemical or mechanical law, without the necessary intervention of any mental influences whatever. This is the great illusion of the materialist.

Imagination, intellect, will, emotion, faith, hope, expectation, etc., are only states or modes of the soul's own life, and they are in perpetual activity, whether we are conscious of it or not. The operations of the soul of which we are not conscious, are almost infinite in comparison with the very small portion of them which comes at any moment within the range of our external consciousness. The soul organizes its own body in the womb of the mother, holds all its parts together in due order and functional activity during life, and when he quits it at death, its material tenement falls into dissolution.

The mind of man is constantly at work, silently pervading every tissue of his body by its vital influence, repeating itself in every func- tion, throbbing in the heart, breathing in the lungs, reflecting itself in the blood, weaving its own form into every act of nutrition, realizing its own life in every sensation, and working its own will in every motion. The power of the mind over the body indeed! There is no power in the body, but in the mind, for the body is the mind, trans- lated into flesh and blood.

When a limb is broken—the bones shattered, the flesh torn, the blood-vessels severed, the nerves lacerated, what can the surgeon or doctor do to repair the injury? A little outside mechanical work. He ligates, he stitches, he plasters, he fixes the parts in apparatus so they will remain motionless in the natural position. He can do no more. The soul which creates the body and keeps it in health, repairs it when injured. By her own occult forces she regulates the movement of the blood and development of nerve power, the chemical decom- position and re-combination, going on in every tissue, according to ideas and models implanted upon her by the Divine Mind, the Over- Soul of the universe.

The old writers call this wonderful power the *vis medicatrix naturi*, the curative power of nature. Swedenborg, for whom nature has no powers underived from spiritual sources, teaches that this vital power is the soul itself. His view that the soul itself acts uncon- sciously to our perceptions in the development and conservation of the body is advocated by Morell in his "Elements of Psychology," and is highly spoken of by Professor William B. Carpenter.

When we have constructed a true psychological pathology, we shall understand clearly why and how it is that fear can turn the hair gray in a single night; that a mother's milk can be poisoned by a moment of terror; that the heart may be paralyzed by a sudden joy or sorrow; that dyspepsia, paralysis, and many other diseases are produced by mental worry and fret and the brain-fag of overwork and anxiety. Yea, we will understand that away back of all physical causation, the roots of our disease originate in the spiritual conditions of the race, in our false religions, our false philosophies, our false way of thinking, our false relations to God and each other.

The most extensive of all the morbid mental conditions which reflect themselves so disastrously on the human system, is the state of fear. It has many degrees or gradations, from the state of extreme alarm, fright, or terror, down to the slightest shade of apprehension of impending evil. But all along the line it is the same thing—a paralyzing impression upon the centers of life which can produce, through the agency of the nervous system, a vast variety of morbid symptoms in every tissue of the body.

We have very seldom reflected upon the fact that fear runs like a baleful thread through the whole web of our life from beginning to end. We are born into the atmosphere of fear and dread, and the mother who bore us had lived in the same atmosphere for weeks and months before we were born. We are surrounded in infancy and childhood by clouds of fear and apprehension on the part of our parents, nurses, and friends. As we advance in life we become, instinctively or by experience, afraid of almost everything. We are afraid of our parents, afraid of our teachers, afraid of our playmates, afraid of ghosts, afraid of rules and regulations and punishments, afraid of the doctor, the dentist, the surgeon. Our adult life is a state of chronic anxiety, which is fear in a milder form. We are afraid of failure in business, afraid of disappointments and mistakes, afraid of enemies, open or concealed; afraid of poverty, afraid of public opinion, afraid of accidents, of sickness, of death, and unhappiness after death. Man is like a haunted animal from the cradle to the grave, the victim of real or imaginary fears, not only his own, but those reflected upon him from the superstitions, self-deceptions, sensory illusions, false beliefs and concrete errors of the whole human race, past and present.

If fear produces disease, acute or chronic, suddenly or gradually, through the correlations existing between the spirit and the body, how can there be a genuinely and perfectly healthy man or woman in the world? There is none.

That fear does produce all kinds of disease, has been frequently observed and fully substantiated by the medical profession. Dr. Tuke, in his admirable book, "Influence of the Mind upon the Body," cites well authenticated instances of the following diseases as having been produced by fear or fright: Insanity, idiocy, paralysis of various muscles and organs, profuse perspirations, cholerina, jaundice, turning of the hair gray in a short time, baldness, sudden decay of the teeth, nervous shock followed by fatal anæmia, uterine troubles, malformation of embryo through the mother, and even skin disease—erysipelas, eczema, and impetigo.

We observe in this list that fear not only affects the mind and the nervous and muscular tissues, but the molecular chemical transformations of the organic network, even to the skin, the hair, and the teeth. This might be expected of a passion which disturbs the whole mind, which is represented or externalized in the whole body.

Dr. Tuke reiterates the fact which has been so frequently observed, that epidemics owe a great deal of their rapid extension and violence to the panic of fear which exists among the people. When yellow fever, cholera, smallpox, diphtheria, and other malignant diseases obtain a footing in a community, hundreds and thousands of people fall victims to their own mental conditions, which invite the attack and insure its fatality. When the disease was new and strange, as the yellow fever was to the interior in its visitation in 1878, when the doctors were not familiar with it, the nurses not trained to it, the people, having no confidence in its management, lost hope, their fears became excessive, and consequent mortality was frightful.

How does fear operate upon the body to produce sickness? By paralyzing the nerve centres, especially those of the vasomotor nerves, thus producing not only muscular relaxation, but capillary congestions of all kinds. This condition of the system invites attack, and there is no resilience, or power of resistance. The gates of the citadel have been opened from within, and the enemy may enter at any point.

What determines the specific nature of the disease which attacks a person thus prostrated by fear? Men are frequently prostrated by fear in storms or fire or earthquakes or accidents, and no disease results. It is because they have been not thinking and brooding over any special morbid conditions. But in an epidemic, say of yellow fever, the subjects connected with the disease are strongly pictured on the mind. They are talked of, read about, discussed and written about, until the mind is full of images of fever, delirium, black vomit, jaundice, death, funerals, etc. When such is the case, no microbes or bacteria are needed to produce an outburst of yellow fever. The whole mass of horrors already stamped upon the mind is simply reflected and repeated in the body.

"As a man thinketh, so is he," said Solomon. Thoughts become things, apprehensions take form and substance, and lo! the disease. In the height of his happiness and prosperity, Job permitted himself to brood in silent fear over the possibility of losses and misfortunes, and he had at last to exclaim, "The thing which I greatly feared has come upon me."

Sudden and great fears are not frequent. The fears of every day, the constant apprehensions and anxieties of life, which are really fears of impending evil, prey upon our vitality and lessen our power of resisting, so that any passing disease may be photographed on our minds and seen upon our bodies.

Fear is itself a contagious disease, and is sometimes reflected from one to another mind with great rapidity. It needs no speech or sign to propagate it, for by psychological laws we are just beginning to comprehend, it passes from one to another, from the healthy to the sick, from the doctor or the nurse to the patient, from the mother to the child. Thus malignant influences may be cast around us by even our best friends and would-be helpers, under whose baleful shadow, without our even knowing of its existence, we and our children may sicken and die.

The summer of 1888 was signalized by a moderately severe epidemic of yellow fever at Jacksonville, Florida, and a very extensive epidemic of fear throughout the Southern states. The latter disease was much more contagious than the former, and much less amenable to treatment. This mental malady visited every little town, village, and railway station, and kept the people in a chill of trepidation for many weeks. This causeless and senseless terror originated many precipitate and unjust measures of self-defense. Under its influence public and private rights were disrespected, and the panic greatly intensified. In a few cases the refugee was driven from the door, the hungry left unfed, the sick unattended. There was exhibited on a small scale, here and there, that same principle of terror which is manifested in a burning theatre, on a sinking ship, or in a stampeded army, when brave men suddenly become cowards, and wise men fools, and merciful men brutes.

Truly, something ought to be done for the moral treatment of yellow fever.

I will relate an anecdote of Dr. Samuel Cartwright, of Natchez, Mississippi, which furnishes an ideal type for the mental treatment of yellow fever.

It was away back in the thirties, and yellow fever was prevailing in New Orleans, and the places above it were in a state of watchful fear. A young Northern teacher, trying to return home, started from Woodville, Mississippi, and arrived at Natchez about midnight in a high fever. Dr. Cartwright was immediately called in. Early in the morning he summoned the officers of the hotel and all the regular boarders into the parlor and made them a little speech. "This young lady," he said, "has yellow fever. It is not contagious. None of you will take it from her; and if you will follow my advice you will save this town from a panic, and a panic is the hotbed of an epidemic. Say nothing about this case. Ignore it absolutely. Let the ladies of the house help nurse her, and take flowers and delicacies to her, and act altogether as if it were some every-day affair, unattended by danger. It will save her life, and perhaps in the long run many others."

It was agreed to by all but one person—a woman, who proceeded to quarantine herself in the most remote room of the establishment. The young teacher got well, and no one was sick in the house but the self-quarantined woman, who took yellow fever from fear, but happily recovered.

By his great reputation and his strong magnetic power, Dr. Cartwright dissipated the fears of those around him, and prevented an epidemic. For this grand appreciation and successful application of a principle—the power of mind and thought over physical conditions, a power just dawning on the perception of the race—he deserves a nobler monument than any we have accorded to heroes and statesmen.

The sanitarians of the present day would think on the contrary that Dr. Cartwright was worthy of condemnation and imprisonment. Dr. Cartwright, however, honestly believed that yellow fever was not a contagious disease. At that time the non-contagionists were numerous, learned, experienced, and respectable. The contagionists, however, finally carried the day in the face of innumerable evidences of non-contagion, which, strangely enough, have now about ceased to exist. Whether they transformed a non-contagious into a contagious disease by repeated and violent asseverations, which played upon and hypnotized the professional and public mind, is a subtle point for psychological investigation, not likely to be made by the present generation of doctors.

Can a non-contagious disease become contagious by mental action? The power of fear to modify the currents of the blood and all the secretions, to whiten the hair, to paralyze the nervous system, and even to produce death is well known. Its power to impress organic changes upon the child in the womb through the mother's mind is well established. When yellow fever is reported about and believed to be imminent and contagious, fear, combined with a vivid imagination of the horrors and woes of the pest, can precipitate sickness which will take on the form and color present to the thought, and yellow fever may spread rapidly from person to person, all through the medium of the mind. "Everything," said a great philosopher, "was at first a thought."

We see a non-contagious disease in the very process of transformation into a contagious one in the case of pulmonary consumption. It was observed occasionally that one of the married partners who had nursed the other through the disease fell a victim after a while to the same malady. Doctors and people began to suggest contagion. The cases of one attack following the other were noticed more and more, and were reported in the medical journals. It was spoken of, thought of, brooded over. The confirmatory cases were all carefully noted; the failures to infect were all ignored, as they always are by people who are looking for contagion. The germ theory has given a great impetus to the idea of contagion. Dr. Loomis actually classifies tuberculosis among miasmatic contagious diseases. Fear will do the rest. In another generation the occasional fact will be a common fact, and in still another, a fixed fact; and the contagiousness of consumption will be enrolled among the concrete errors of the profession. Such has probably been the genesis of all contagious diseases in the remote past.

Fear being recognized as a powerful cause of disease, and a direct and great obstacle to recovery, a wise sanitation will exert itself to prevent or antidote its influences. To eradicate fear is to avert disease, to shorten its duration, diminish its virulence, and promote recovery. How shall we accomplish it? By educating the people up to a higher standard of life. By teaching them a sounder hygiene, a wiser philosophy, a more cheerful theology. By erasing a thousand errors, delusions, and superstitions from their minds, and giving instead the light, the beauty, and the loveliness of truth. There is a mental and moral sanitation ahead of us, which is far more valuable and desirable than all our quarantines, inventions, experimentations, and microscopic search for physical causes.

I will draw the picture of a sick room in charge of physicians and nurse, by whom this enlighted sanitation has been ignored or unheeded. It is a chamber of fear, soon, in all probability, to be the chamber of death. The room is darkened, for they are afraid of the light, that emblem of God's wisdom which should shine into all rooms, except when it is disagreeable to the patient. The ventilation is insufficient, for draughts, you must know, are very dangerous. The friends have doleful faces, moist eyes, sad voices, which reveal danger and doubt, and they converse in subdued whispers, which alarm and annoy the patient. The nurse and the doctor sometimes talk of their cases before the sick man, tell how very ill they were, how they suffered, how they got well miraculously, or how they died. The sympathetic visitor regales his hearers, the patient included, with his or her knowledge of similar cases, and their results, the great amount of sickness prevailing, and the success or ill success of this or that doctor.

They all agree that it is dangerous to change the patient's linen, dangerous to sponge the body, dangerous to give him cold water; milk is feverish, meat is too strong. A shadow of fear seems to hang over everybody. The pulse is counted, the temperature is taken. Nurse or nearest friend wants to know aloud the report of the watch and the thermometer. The doctor answers aloud, and all look grave. And so it goes on day after day, thoughts and images of pain and sickness and danger and death being impressed and reflected upon the mind of the patient, and the great, sound, glorious spirit within finds it impossible to break through this dense atmosphere of material superstitions, fear, ignorance, and folly, and restore its own body to health and happiness.

The true sanitarian will remember in his treatment the tremendous power of words and ideas upon the sick. He will never indicate by his language, his looks, or his conduct that he thinks the patient is very ill. He will cleanse his own mind of morbid fears and apprehensions, and reflect the stimulating light of hope on all around him. The suppression of anxiety, and even sometimes of sympathy, is necessary. His sickness should not be discussed before the patient, or any other case of sickness alluded to. The doctor's opinion of the case should never be asked, and never given within the patient's hearing. Erase, as far as possible, all thoughts of disease, danger, or death. The sick-room should not be darkened and made silent. It should be made cheerful and natural, as if no sickness existed. It should have fresh air, and cool water, and the fragrance of flowers, instead of the odor of drugs. Hope, and not fear, should be the presiding genius of the place.

The mind-curers and the Christian Scientists say that almost all acute diseases can be cured without medicine by the simple dissipation of fear from the mind of the patient, of his friends, and of his doctor. Whether this be true or not, it is very certain that when an epidemic is threatened or prevailing, the people who are constantly talking about and discussing the disease, the newspapers which daily report its progress and fatality, and the doctors and nurses who ventilate their experiences, who predict evil, speak ominously and enjoin all sorts of precautions, are themselves fomenters and carriers of the disease, infectious centers to the whole community.

Education can do much, but it is useless to expect the total eradication of fear without the aid and guidance of the religious principle. Fear is the cry of the wounded selfhood for something he has suffered or lost, or is about to lose. "Perfect love casteth out fear"— the perfect love of God and the neighbor. He who is in bondage to the senses has everything to dread. He alone is free from all apprehensions whose heart and mind are stayed upon the living God. He truly "sits under his own vine and fig-tree, with none to make him afraid."

MR. KENNAN'S APPRENTICESHIP IN COURAGE

MR. George Kennan's great work in Russian exploration and in the investigation of Russian institutions has been due to certain qualities of character which impress every one who knows him well. Of these qualities, bravery and strength of will are not the least conspicuous. In his conversations with me, he has often spoken of certain things in connection with his own development and training, which are of much interest. Once when I spoke to him of his bravery and coolness under danger, he said:—

"Many things which have been significant and controlling in what I may call my psychological life are wholly unknown to my friends, and yet they might be made public, if you wish. For instance, as I look back to my boyhood, the cause of the only unhappiness that boyhood had for me was a secret but a deeply rooted suspicion that I was physically a coward. This gave me intense suffering. I do not know precisely at what time I first became conscious of it, but when I peered, one day, through the window of a surgeon's office to see an amputation I had proof of my fear. One of my playmates had caught his hand between two cog-wheels in a mill, and his arm had been badly crushed. When he was taken to the surgeon's office, I followed to see what was going to be done with him. While I was watching the amputation, with my face pressed to the glass of the window, the surgeon accidentally let slip from his forceps the end of one of the severed arteries, and a jet of blood spurted against the inside of the window-pane. The result upon me was a sensation that I had never had before in all my life,—a sensation of nausea, faintness, and overwhelming fear. I was twenty-four hours in recovering from the shock, and from that time I began to think about the nature of my emotions and the unsuspected weakness of my character.

”I had a nervous, imaginative temperament, and not long after this incident I began to be tortured by a vague suspicion that I was lacking in what we now call ‘nerve,’ that I was afraid of things that involved suffering or peril. I brooded over this suggestion of physical cowardice until I became almost convinced of its reality, and at last I came to be afraid of things that I had never before thought about. In less than a year I had lost much of my self-respect, and was as miserable as a boy could be. It all seems now very absurd and childish, but at that time, with my boyish visions of travel and exploration, it was a spiritual tragedy. ‘Of what use is it to think of exploration and wild life in wild countries,’ I used to ask myself, ‘if the first time my courage or fortitude is put to the test I become faint and sick?’

“I began at last to experiment upon myself,—to do things that were dangerous merely to see whether I dared do them; but the result was only partially reassuring. I could not get into much danger in a sleepy little village like Norwalk, Ohio, and although I found I could force myself to walk around the six-inch stone coping of a bell-tower five stories from the ground (a most perilous and foolhardy exploit), and go and sit alone in a graveyard in the middle of dark, still nights, I failed to recover my own respect. My self-reproach continued for a year or two, during which I was as wretched as a boy can be who admires courage above all things and has a high ideal of intrepid manhood, but who secretly fears that he himself is hopelessly weak and nerveless. There was hardly a day that I did not say to myself, ‘You’ll never be able to do the things that you dream about; you haven’t any self-reliance or nerve. Even as a little child you were afraid of the dark; you shrink now from fights and rows, and you turn faint at the mere sight of blood. You’re nothing but a coward.’

“At last, when I was seventeen or eighteen years of age, I went to

Cincinnati as a telegraph operator. I had become so morbid and miserable by that time that I said one day, 'I'm going to put an end to this state of affairs here and now. If I'm afraid of anything, I'll conquer my fear of it or die. If I'm a coward I might as well be dead, because I can never feel any self-respect or have any happiness in life; and I'd rather get killed trying to do something that I'm afraid to do than to live in this way.' I was at that time working at night, and had to go home from the office between midnight and four o'clock A. M. It was during the Civil War, and Cincinnati was a more lawless city than it has ever been since. Street robberies and murders were of daily occurrence, and all of the 'night men' in our office carried weapons as a matter of course. I bought a revolver, and commenced a course of experiments upon myself. When I finished my night work at the office, instead of going directly home through well-lighted and police-patrolled streets, I directed my steps to the slums and explored the worst haunts of vice and crime in the city. If there was a dark, narrow, cut-throat alley down by the river that I felt afraid to go through at that hour of the night, I clenched my teeth, cocked my revolver, and went through it,—sometimes twice in succession. If I read in the morning papers that a man had been robbed or murdered on a certain street, I went to that street the next night. I explored the dark river-banks, hung around low drinking-dives and the resorts of thieves and other criminals, and made it an invariable rule to do at all hazards the thing that I thought I might be afraid to do. Of course I had all sorts of experiences and adventures. One night I saw a man attacked by highwaymen and knocked down with a slung-shot, just across the street. I ran to his assistance, frightened away the robbers, and picked him up from the gutter in a state of unconsciousness. Another night, after two o'clock, I saw a man's throat cut, down by the river,—and a ghastly sight it was; but, although somewhat shaken, I did not become faint or sick. Every time I went through a street that I believed to be dangerous, or had any startling experience, I felt an accession of self-respect.

"In less than three months I had satisfied myself that while I did feel fear, I was not so much daunted by any undertaking but I could do it if I willed to do it, and then I began to feel better.

"Not long after this I went on my first expedition to Siberia, and there, in almost daily struggles with difficulties, dangers, and sufferings of all sorts, I finally lost the fear of being afraid which had poisoned the happiness of my boyhood. It has never troubled me, I think, since the fall of 1867, when I was blown out to sea one cold and pitch-dark night in a dismasted and sinking sailboat, in a heavy, offshore gale, without a swallow of water or a mouthful of food. I faced then for about four hours what seemed to be certain death, but I was steady, calm, and under perfect self-control."

—Kenyon West.

Advertisement of "Menticulture."

"MENTICULTURE" was first issued in a sufficiently modest way. It described a personal experience which has been of inestimable value to the author. The revelation to him of the possibility of the absolute elimination of the seeds of unhappiness has changed life from a period of constant struggle to a period of security and repose, and has insured delightful realities instead of uncertain possibilities. One hundred and fifty copies of the book were privately printed, and entitled "The A B C of True Living." It also carried within its pages the title of "Emancipation."

The suggestion met with such hearty appreciation on the part of personal friends in many various walks of life, that a public edition was proposed, and the name of "Menticulture," a name that had to be coined for the purpose, was chosen for it.

The aptness of the suggestion has been evidenced by the approval of the brotherhood at large by appreciative notices in many of the leading periodicals of the country, by the receipt of more than a thousand personal letters by the author, many of them attesting to greatest benefits growing out of the new point of view of life suggested by the book, and by very large sales.

One gentleman—altruist—whose name is W. J. Van Patten, found the suggestion contained in "Menticulture" so helpful to himself and friends that he purchased a special edition of two thousand copies of the book for distribution in his home city of Burlington, Vermont, one to each household, with the idea of accentuating the suggestion by widespread inter-discussion. The special Burlington edition has an inset page bearing Mr. Van Patten's *raison d'être* for the distribution, which reads as follows:

PERSONAL NOTE

Some time in the early part of the year 1896 a friend sent me a copy of "Menticulture." I read it with interest, and became convinced that I could apply its truths to my own life with profit. Experience confirmed my faith in the power of its principles to overcome many of the most annoying and damaging ills that are common to humanity.

I procured a number of copies from time to time and gave to friends who I felt would appreciate it. The universal testimony to the good which the little book did, and the new strength of purpose and will it gave to some who were sore beset with the cares and worries of life, increased my interest and my confidence in the truths set forth.

I formed the idea of making an experiment by giving the book a general distribution in our city, to see if it would not promote the general good and happiness of people.

I wrote to the author, Mr. Fletcher, and he entered into the plan very cordially, and had this special edition prepared for me. The object which we hope to gain is to turn the thoughts and purposes of those whom we reach to the old truths taught by Christ, and a determination to live above those evils which do so much to make our lives unhappy for ourselves and annoying to those about us.

I would ask, therefore, that you would kindly give the book careful and thoughtful reading, and, when you have opportunity, recommend it to your friends.

W. J. Van Patten.

Mr. Van Patten is a prominent manufacturer of Vermont, and was recently Mayor of Burlington for two years. He is also prominent in the Christian Endeavorer movement, having been the first president of the United Society, and being at present one of its trustees, as well as the president of the Congregational Club of western Vermont.

"Menticulture" has found favor among physicians, and also with life-insurance companies, obviously because of the live-saving quality of the suggestions contained in it.